Careers in Film and Video

RICKI OSTROV AND HOWARD HALL

FIFTH EDITION

KOGAN PAGE
CAREERS
SERIES

First published in 1984, entitled *Careers in the Film Industry*,
by Ricki Ostrov
Second edition 1989, entitled *Careers in Film and Video*,
by Ricki Ostrov and Bill McCoid
Third edition 1992 by Ricki Ostrov and Alison King
Fourth edition 1994 by Ricki Ostrov and Howard Hall
Fifth edition 1996

Kogan Page Limited
120 Pentonville Road
London N1 9JN

© Kogan Page Limited 1984, 1989, 1992, 1994, 1996

British Library Cataloguing in Publication Data

A CIP record for this book is available from the
British Library.

ISBN 0-7494-1929-6

Typeset by DP Photosetting, Aylesbury, Bucks
Printed and bound in Great Britain by
Clays Ltd, St Ives plc

Contents

Introduction

There can be few careers with a more glamorous, exciting and fun image than working in the film and video industry. At least, that's how it appears from the outside! The downside is that the competition is about as tough as it comes and you will often work long and hard at unsocial hours, with a tendency for your work to take over your life. This can sound very romantic and thrilling but the reality soon sorts out the people who genuinely want to do it from those who just 'fancied' it. If all you like is the image and the idea of working in glamorous jobs, you'd better know now the price you have to pay.

There is a classic catch 22 situation in the industry: you cannot get a job without experience and without a job you never get experience. If you cannot find a way round this problem you can forget about working in the film and video industry. There is always a way in if you try hard enough, and if you cannot find a way, then you are not determined enough for the industry.

Another industry myth is that everyone gets paid vast sums of money for doing very little. When you first start working you will probably not get paid at all or will be poorly paid as a runner or general dogsbody just to get experience and see how the industry works. Once you are in and you are keen, willing and able, you can ask questions, watch, look and learn from the more experienced crew members. Working with people in the industry is your chance to learn and impress; if you don't use the opportunities you will not last long.

People will help you if you ask them and will often be generous with their time, but don't expect them to behave like teachers. It's up to you - they will not volunteer the information unless you seem keen to get it, because they have better things to do with their time.

The industry does place a high price on practical experience and 'going through the mill'. Everyone will ask to see what you have done and will then ask how you did it. Theory does not count for much; practical experience does.

Having said this, a good course at a recognised film school or college can open doors for you, but you must ensure that the course covers practical skills of production and is not just film theory and criticism, unless you want to be a critic or a teacher of theory. But whatever the area of film and video, learning what quality is takes hard study, practical craft and experimentation.

What are the Qualities You Need?

Talent, determination, luck, professionalism, marketing skills, enthusiasm. I can go on listing characteristics all day but you must analyse your own character and look at your own strengths and weaknesses.

The big question is, do you know what you want to do? Once you are sure you can answer this question and that you have answered it realistically, truthfully and honestly and not just 'wished upon a star', then life gets much simpler. With the decision made you can devise a realistic plan of how to achieve your aim and what steps you must take to achieve each phase. Again, be realistic and don't fool yourself. Can you get the qualifications, contacts or experience needed, and are you prepared to forgo other pleasures in life to achieve your goals? Don't believe the press articles about young people suddenly being given a massive film to make – life is not like the movies.

Creativity and Organisation

If the industry appeals to the creative side of your nature and you believe that whizzing about with a camera or hanging around studios is what is called for, you will be disappointed. You need to be highly organised and be able to plan with meticulous detail. Every film and video should be planned like a military operation, so if you get your bit wrong it's the firing squad! It is a puzzle why the creative side of the British film and video industry is so skilled and well organised, yet the business and finance side is such a mess. This has always been where the USA has got its act together. Happily, things are changing and there is potential for funding from the European Union, both for business and production.

Find Out What You Like Doing Best – Then get somebody to pay you to do it!

This advice tells you the ideal situation, but both halves of it are difficult to follow. If you have got as far as reading this book, you are obviously interested in a career in the film and video business and want some help to get someone to pay you to do it.

So what are your chances? Well, good connections in the industry can be an advantage, but because the communications industry is predicted to be a growth area there should be more opportunities for people who are prepared to work hard. Still, full-time employment is becoming scarcer within the industry, which is now more geared to the freelance market, meaning that you may have long periods without work. There had to be a catch somewhere. Also, nobody will hire a freelance trainee, so you have to learn your trade before they will use you.

Film, TV and Independent Video Companies

To begin with, the independent video industry didn't make programmes for showing in cinema theatres or on televisions. The sector was looked down on by the main players in film and TV, who regarded it as amateurish and irrelevant. But the sector proved itself a very prosperous business, and by the mid 1980s big and small companies, the government, local authorities and record companies were all using the medium to promote and inform. For example, John Cleese, with Video Arts, tapped into this market and made a fortune from programmes on management techniques.

The independents quickly became experts in production techniques, often leaving behind the old guard of television who hadn't looked over their shoulders to see what was going on. Polished presenters and graphics techniques utilising all the new equipment and skills were the everyday tools of production in the corporate video world. Pop videos blew away the old world of TV production: they broke all the rules and people loved it. Thus the walls began to crumble, just as they had between film and television. This meant that there was a new entry route into the industry; a new place to learn your skills and become expert enough to move freely between film, TV and non-broadcast.

Satellite

The satellite revolution has had little lasting impact on the country's production industry, with most of the jobs being on the marketing and sales side rather than in actually making programmes or films. The merging of BSB with Sky virtually killed off production of programmes specifically for satellite transmission, and most of their material is now bought in cheaply from the USA.

However, they do make some news and current affairs programmes that employ journalists, presenters and writers, and they do look for enthusiasm and commitment rather than just experience when they take people on. They also employ script runners who can get hands-on experience and then, if they show promise, can work their way up into a skilled job.

Cable

These are essentially delivery companies rather than being production orientated. By 1995 there were about 125 cable franchises in operation. Most of the cable companies transmit many of the satellite channels and also make studio-based programmes of local interest, so it can be a useful training ground for studio operations.

Getting Qualified

Qualifications and The Film Industry

Very often it is whether you are 'in' the industry that matters and not qualifications, which are sometimes seen as completely irrelevant. Traditionally, the crafts were handed down to those in the industry, with no chance for anyone outside to learn. Being a runner was the only way in, even with a degree. It meant long hours, low pay and menial work, and even then only the most persistent got in.

Entry is not so restricted now, although people are still expected to start at the bottom. Despite its drawbacks it gives the opportunity to gain experience of how the industry works. It also allows people in the industry to assess the suitability and aptitude of a new recruit. Unless they are judged to be dedicated and determined and to have the aptitude for the work, they will not last as a runner: for these are the essential qualities of the industry. This can be seen as a stupid and restrictive system but it has worked and the people that come through it are the best in the world. Nobody is let loose in a job until they can do it; this prevents expensive mistakes.

Qualifications and Television

Television tends to be very different from other sectors of the industry. Academic qualifications are important and are essential for top-level grades such as producer or director. But journalism can be another route in, via a job as a researcher and then training to higher grades.

If technology is your bag, then television engineering could be for you. This is now also tending towards the degree side and constant re-training is also needed. Unfortunately, the training side of the BBC and ITV has taken a back seat and may not survive at all in the future. Increasing reliance on freelancers has led to a skill shortage in some areas which is now being addressed by organisations such as Skillset and FT2 (see pages 30–31, 66 and 74).

Degrees

If you are looking for a key to unlock the door you won't find one just by having a degree. It may help you get a foot in the door but it won't necessarily open it for you. The industry was strongly biased towards on-the-job training but now nobody can afford to train people, so often only expert freelances are employed: another catch 22.

Many media courses once completely ignored any technical training and looked down on people getting their hands dirty. Technical ability was considered a handcap to the intellectual process. This attitude is changing as people realise that it produces people who understand the process, can argue and criticise well, but can't make programmes. Whenever you choose a course, always ask how this course will provide you with the skills and knowledge that you will need in order to do what you want to do. If you haven't got the skills, you won't get the job.

Some universities have a better reputation and better facilities than others, so choose your course carefully. If there isn't the equipment available you won't be able to experiment with it. Also check out the course tutors. Have they had any practical experience of actually making films and videos in the professional world or are they academics? Look for work placements and staff to student ratios.

Drama and art degrees will still have some relevance in their particular areas and computer literacy is a useful additional skill.

National Vocational Qualifications (NVQs)

The way in which training is given within the industry is undergoing major changes as the system of National Vocational Qualifications (NVQs) and Scottish Vocational Qualifications (SVQs) is introduced. NVQs and SVQs are designed to make sure that a person can do a job, demonstrating competence in a given role to industry standards, and not just talk or write about it. Assessments are carried out either in an actual place of work or in a training centre designed to match work conditions.

NVQ and SVQ awards are given at five levels, ranging from basic skills to high levels of professional ability. Levels 2, 3 and 4 are already being developed for film and video, and development of level 5 will commence in the near future.

When developing NVQs and SVQs, professionals in the relevant industry sectors are consulted so that the expected standards for NVQs and SVQs will reflect the requirements of the industry. All NVQs for film and video will be administered, awarded and monitored by Skillset and the Open University Validation Service or, in Scotland, by Skillset and SCOTVEC. RSA, BTEC and City and Guilds all support the NVQ programme.

In addition, there are General National Vocational Qualifications (GNVQs), which teach a mix of academic and vocational skills. The GNVQ course entitled *Media: Communications and Production* is available at Intermediate or Advanced Level at several colleges around Britain, details of which are published in full in *Media Courses UK* (1996), published by the British Film Institute at £9.95.

If you get the 'bug' you'll want to work in the industry for ever. If not you'll soon be disenchanted and be off to find something else. Temperament and character have as much to do with working in the industry as qualifications; attitude is important and emotions can run high on a shoot. Could you stand being blamed and bawled at for something that was not your fault, and still bounce back? Big money is at stake and people want results, not excuses.

Remember to enjoy yourself while you're working because it's more a way of life than a job.

Part 1

Chapter 1

The Structure of the Industry

Organisation

The film industry, located mostly in London, consists mainly of production companies, studios, post-production houses and film distributors.

Production companies, of which there are hundreds around London, actually produce the films. They usually have one or more in-house producers and directors, a secretary or personal assistant, a receptionist and a messenger. The number of permanent staff of most production companies is kept to a minimum, with the technical staff needed for each production being hired on a freelance basis.

The studios, such as Shepperton and Pinewood, do not produce films any more – they do not have permanent film-makers on staff. They are what is known as 'four-walled', letting space and facilities to production companies who usually bring their own crew with them. Some companies are located at the studio full time and others relocate themselves at the studio when they are using the facilities for filming.

The post-production sector of the industry includes the film laboratories and a number of companies providing a variety of services, including editing rooms, film sound recording studios, opticals and special effects.

Film distributors handle the marketing and publicity for films as well as coordinating the physical distribution of film prints to cinemas and screening rooms. Most of the staff are clerical.

Films

We usually think of films as having huge budgets, large, all-star casts and lots of publicity. But there are a number of different types of films, used for a variety of purposes, being made today.

Feature films are those which are specifically intended for cinema release. They are full length, about 110 minutes, and are generally fiction. Because the cost of filming can be high, sometimes running into millions of pounds, there are few British feature films being made. Most of the features shot in Britain are American-financed and produced. Independent productions are usually made on a much smaller budget and are shorter. These include movies for both cinema and television viewing, and television programmes including documentaries and shorts.

The making of commercials for television is another area of activity. Although broadcast on television, most commercials are shot on film and then transferred to tape. This is also the case for most pop videos.

There is a wide range of films not intended for commercial or broadcasting purposes. These include government educational and training films, industrial or scientific films and material used for marketing and public relations.

Films are usually more up-market productions than videos, not least because they cost more to make. However, this should not put you off; there is a current trend towards the 'just do it' school which is to be applauded. It is symptomatic of the new, independent breed of film makers in this country who get on with making the films they want to make without feeling that they need to have massive resources behind them.

Finance

Raising the money to make a movie can often be the most difficult part of film-making. To begin with, there are a number of government institutions with small sums available for British productions. The 1985 Films Act ended the Eady Levy and the National Film Finance Corporation, which it helped to fund. It was replaced by the British Screen Finance Consortium, which is funded by the government, Pathé Screen Entertainment, Granada TV, Rank and Channel 4. The Consortium finances British film-makers who meet certain requirements.

British Screen supports British film makers seeking to develop and produce films for the cinema by providing commercial loans for specific projects. At present between £4 million and £5 million is available annually to fund projects. It helps to finance between 10 and 12 feature films every year, usually providing about 20 per cent of the production budget. There is also a European Co-production Fund (ECF) financed by a government grant to assist British producers making co-productions with partners in other EU countries.

A number of private investment corporations have been set up specifically to raise money to finance films. Although many City investors were once reluctant to invest in film-making since it is such a high risk, a change in tax laws and the international success of British films such as *Chariots of Fire* and *Gandhi* and, more recently, *Four Weddings and a Funeral* and *Trainspotting*, have made money-raising a little easier.

There are a number of other methods of raising money, including selling television and foreign distribution rights, selling the rights to video sales, guarantees against royalties and deals with American studios and distributors.

Probably the most important source of finance is Channel 4. Though their budget is not the largest, it is consistent and provides a stable funding base, something the industry has been without for a long time. In addition to the monies provided for productions intended for television, Channel 4 also finances British feature films. Often these are shown in cinemas for a specific length of time and are then broadcast on television.

Chapter 2

Working in the Industry

Personal Qualities

If you asked someone in the film industry what quality you needed to succeed, the answer would most often be perseverance. Because of the structure of the industry you have to realise that reaching your goal may take years. You need to be willing to continue after many rejections and you have to accept that there may be long periods of unemployment. You need a strong will, a lot of determination, and you need to love what you are doing.

When working on a production, you have to be able to function as a member of a team, to take instructions and directions. You will often have to work long hours, including evenings and weekends, sometimes in bad weather. You need to stay calm under pressure, be creative and open to new ideas and suggestions.

Breaking into the film industry is not easy, no matter how much training you have. There is a lot of competition for jobs and many times when you have finished one job you are immediately out looking for another. You need to be aggressive, adaptable and determined. You have to keep trying – without that determination and perseverance, your chances of succeeding are low.

The Stages of Film-making

There are three steps in film-making, each involving different groups of people. Some may be involved in only one stage, some are involved in all three.

Pre-production. This is the stage when all the components are organised in preparation for actual filming. The producer first finds the story or comes up with the concept of the film and he/she will then obtain the financing for the production. During pre-production the director is hired, the film is cast and the crew assembled. A typical crew will include jobs such as cameraman/woman, director of photography, production manager, designer, location manager, production runner, production buyer, property master, gaffer, first, second and third assistant, script supervisor, boom operator, art director and set dresser. Locations and equipment are also arranged. A budget and a shooting schedule are prepared, and these are often the responsibility of the production manager.

Production. This is the actual filming or 'shooting' of the picture. It is done either on location or in a studio. Normally, the majority of jobs are actively involved in this stage.

Post-production. The film is processed by a laboratory, edited and then completed. Editing involves not only cutting the picture, but adding the sound track, opticals (manipulation of images), titles and special effects. This stage may take longer than the actual filming, especially on feature films, pop videos or television commercials.

Job Descriptions

The roles and responsibilities of many involved in making a film often overlap and coincide, depending on the type of film being made. Feature films tend to have a much larger crew with several assistants. Documentaries tend to keep the crew down to a minimum. Few technicians have the luxury of working only in one area of film-making – most will do a number of films in one year, including commercials, possibly a feature, and two or three independent productions. A general guide to the jobs available in film-making is given below.

Producer

The producer is the member of the film unit who controls the organisation and finances, and who is the final authority on all practical matters. He/she usually comes up with the idea for the film, obtains the rights to the property if it is a book or script, or oversees the writing of an original screenplay. The producer is also responsible for obtaining the finance. He/she hires the director and is involved in casting, finding locations and hiring the crew. The producer holds the purse strings, making certain that the film can be completed on the amount of money available. The producer puts the entire package together and then monitors the day-to-day progress of the film.

A good producer will be interested in a variety of subjects and is always coming up with new ideas for production. He/she should be determined, almost totally unreasonable at times, and unwilling to take 'no' for an answer. A producer needs to be able to organise more than one job at a time.

Very few producers start out with the intention of producing. Many come from law or business or were originally agents, and a number of producers start their careers as production managers or assistant directors.

Case Studies
Genny is a *producer*.

> I was a housewife and mother before working in film. My husband is a cameraman, so I knew a lot about the business and most of our friends worked in film.
>
> When my husband set up a production company, I wanted to be involved. I offered to do anything and ended up doing secretarial work and keeping the books. I became more and more involved, helping in different areas and learning how a production actually comes together. I knew how much films cost to make and where the money was spent.
>
> Then a friend asked me to produce a promotional film for him on a tight budget. After that, I made more and more films and eventually set up my own company.
>
> I believe strongly that there is room for more new and creative people in film. I always try and give beginners an opportunity to work on a production. It's important for them to understand what happens on a set and how films are made. If somebody writes to me, and is knowledgeable about what I'm doing, and shows enthusiasm and interest, then I'll find the time to talk to them. I can't always offer a job, but I can give some advice and help.
>
> Although I didn't realise it, being a housewife gave me a lot of the experience needed by a good producer. When you manage a home, you control and budget the money; you learn how to make it stretch. You have to organise a lot of people and activities and you need to have a lot of patience, something most mothers have in abundance. We also have a sense about other people – when to placate and when to persist. A producer has to be able to get what he or she wants without offending other people.
>
> It isn't difficult to become a producer but there is so little training that makes any sense. Producing is usually more on the management than creative side of film-making.
>
> Being a female producer, you have to be remarkably tough. You're dealing with men and money – two powerful components – and you will need to be aggressive to get what you want.

Sandra is a *producer*.

It's very much a self-motivated industry. Nobody comes to you. If you want to do something in films, you have just got to go out and do it, and you can only do it if you are obsessed. Self-motivation and obsession are the two most important qualities needed. After that comes a belief in yourself and in the people you are working with. And then comes the ability to bluff – to pick up the phone and ring up anyone, as if you're David Puttnam. And with that, of course, goes that other very important quality – being very thick-skinned.

I came in through the art school system, where I did stage design. From there I went to the English National Opera, where I did literally anything: running round, helping with the costumes, assisting on the sets, even doing the shopping. After ENO I went to work for a theatrical costumiers, Berners and Nathan, and it was there that I first found myself involved in films, meeting the designers, talking to the actors, getting the costumes out. That way I became friendly with quite a few people working on commercials. Soon I was taking my portfolio round to the production companies, getting myself known. I was asked to work on some of Alan Parker's advertising films, as an assistant in the costume department, and soon I was working on some drama-documentaries.

Probably the most useful thing I did was to join AIP, the Association of Independent Producers [now part of PACT, the Producers Alliance for Cinema and Television]. It sounds very high-powered and at first I was very nervous. But they were all terribly helpful and friendly, and after a while – talking to people whom I met through AIP – I realised that there wasn't anything to be frightened about. In fact, many of the other members seemed far less street-wise than me. They have been an enormous help. They run seminars, workshops and surgeries where you can talk to two or three experienced people about what you are doing. But probably the most important thing of all that AIP does is that it gives you a chance to meet other people doing the same sort of thing as you – it gives you contacts.

Contacts count 100 per cent. Start off with an idea; even if you do not get that project off the ground, it opens doors and gives you something to talk about to other people. It means that you have something to offer, and it gives you experience in dealing with production companies, moneymen, agents, etc. All this means more contacts, and the importance of contacts cannot be overstressed. It means, at times, learning the hard way, but in films the hard way is the best way. It might seem incredibly difficult, but you need to have the mentality of someone doing a jigsaw puzzle; if I can do this then I can do that then I can do the other, etc. If you don't have that kind of mind, don't become a producer.

As far as getting a project off the ground goes, the one golden rule is to work with experienced people, particularly to have a lawyer who understands money. All too often an inexperienced director will work with an inexperienced producer and an inexperienced script-writer ... and then they wonder why their project never gets off the ground.

The other golden rule is to make a very good presentation. I'm absolutely horrified at the way I have seen people present things. Recently someone sent me a script and the presentation was absolutely appalling. It wasn't properly typed, the pages were out of order and it was grubby and dirty. It wasn't even in a folder. After a dozen pages I couldn't be bothered to read any more. It may have been brilliant, though it wasn't, but I just couldn't be bothered.

A good presentation is properly typed and put in a neat folder. It has a neat two-page synopsis, a proper budget breakdown and clear and concise CVs. It is properly packaged and contains no surplus words. After all, the presentation is a test. If you can't get a presentation together, there is no chance that you'll ever be able to get a film together.

Director

The director is responsible for deciding how best to use the technical and artistic resources available. He/she is in charge of directing both the actors and the camera; he/she decides how the film will be mapped out and how best to interpret the script for the camera. The director guides the actors on their interpretation of the part and tells the cameraman/woman what kind of image he/she is looking for. It is vitally important for a director to understand the available resources, such as cameras and lenses, lights and the editing process. A director should have good structural and visual sense. He/she should be able to conceptualise a script and visualise it. Directors need to know what they want to say and how best to say it, using certain images, effects and sounds. The director is in complete charge of the studio or location floor and controls the film artistically, having the final say on all creative matters. The responsibilities of the producer and director sometimes overlap, and often clash. Generally, if the two work well together a production will function smoothly.

Case Study
Sarah is a *documentary director*.

> I fell into film-making through television. After graduating, I got a job at a television station as a researcher. The station gave three of us a chance to direct a film which would be broadcast. After that, they expected us to go on with our old jobs. I knew that I couldn't, and that I wanted to be a freelance director. So I went off on my own.

I only direct projects I'm interested in, often producing them as well. I can't see the point of being hired in just to tell the cameras what to do. I am not a director who can be hired out to direct other people's ideas. I want to be able to see the content and the visualisation of my projects through shooting and editing.

I prefer doing documentaries because of the human contact involved, and the chance it gives you to relate to other people. Documentaries involve a lot of contact with real people and social issues. For documentary work, you need to be able to talk, listen and interpret what other people are saying. You give as much as you get. Documentaries are doubly satisfying because you can make a statement – you can educate as well as entertain.

Continuity

The person in charge of continuity is often called the 'script girl', as most of the people responsible for continuity are women. It is a very important job, and involves making certain that everything, from position of props and clothing to gestures and voice inflections, matches from one shot to the next. The script girl (or boy) is responsible for the physical continuity of the film. She works closely with the director, reminding him/her of technical matters, and keeps detailed notes of each shot. For instance, if an actor's jacket collar is turned up in one shot, she makes sure it looks the same in the next. She is there to ensure that the film looks as if it was shot all at once. A script girl needs a highly developed sense of observation, and must be able to notice even the tiniest discrepancy. Part of the job is to keep a detailed log of each day's work, including how long each shot took, how many retakes were needed and notes on what problems occurred.

Production Manager

The production manager is responsible for the overall organisation of the picture under the producer. He/she is, in effect, the producer's deputy and is actively involved in the day-to-day problems of filming. It is the production manager's job to prepare a detailed budget for shooting during pre-production and a shooting schedule based on that budget. The production manager works closely with both the producer and the director.

Once in production, the production manager supervises the smooth running of the shoot, and is responsible for such things as contracts being completed correctly, the hiring of equipment and obtaining permission to film in certain locations. He/she often acts on behalf of the producer. It is the production manager's responsibility to ensure that the film comes in on time and under budget, using the resources in the most efficient manner possible.

Assistant Director

There are usually three assistant directors: a first, second and third. Although called assistant directors, they work more closely with the production department. The first assistant does help the director, but is not the deputy except in crowd scenes.

The first assistant anticipates and carries out the director's practical requirements. He/she supervises the discipline and general organisation of the daily shooting schedule, prepares the call sheets, and liaises with the production manager to make sure the technical needs for the following day's shooting are met. The first assistant is an important link between the production department and the director, often conveying requests from one side to the other. He/she will, however, usually go on to become a production manager rather than a director.

The first assistant will usually hire a second and a third to make a team, choosing people he/she feels comfortable working with. The second and third assistants help the first in his/her role. The second assistant usually works more closely with the production office, preparing for the following day's or week's shooting, making sure the cast and equipment needed are ready and available. The third assistant works on the set, and is responsible for ensuring that the artists receive their call and are on the set when needed. He/she helps keep the production running smoothly, and functions very much as the legs of the first assistant.

The assistant directors are responsible for keeping a good working atmosphere on the set, and are responsible to both crew and cast. They are often a barometer of the crew's feelings, letting the director know when the crew are tired or dissatisfied. They are there to maximise the efficiency of the film unit, to foresee and predict problems and to make certain everything comes together for filming with no time being wasted.

Case Study
Bill is an *assistant director*.

> I got my first job through a friend who was a production secretary. She called and asked if I wanted to be a runner on a feature film. A runner is basically an errand boy, getting cups of tea, delivering

scripts, photocopying – any little thing that has to be done. At that point, during filming, I knew exactly what I wanted to do. It was like a book being opened – a revelation.

Getting the first job was easy. But getting the second job was much harder. When I started working I thought I knew everything, but I now realise how little I actually did know. I didn't take advantage of the people I met and the experience I was gaining.

At the time I started, you had to work as a runner for something like 100 days a year for two or three years before you could apply for a union job. That period is supposed to be your training. You learn about how films are made, what it's like working on a production, what the chain of command is and what each member of the crew does.

Being a runner on a feature film is a great chance to learn. Often you are allowed to do a bit more than just being a runner, experiencing different areas of production. The chance to learn is unbeatable. I also worked as a runner during pre-production and learned how films are planned and put together.

Working in films is hard – I don't think most people realise this. The hours are long, lots of night shooting during cold, terrible weather. This isn't in any way a nine-to-five job. It takes over your whole life. You become totally absorbed in what you're doing and can't really think about day-to-day living. I can't imagine working in any other career. I love music a lot, and have been lucky enough to work on films that combine the two. That seems to be the best of both worlds.

Lighting Cameraman/woman

The person doing this job is often called the cinematographer or director of photography. Apart from the director, he/she is the most creative member of the team. He/she works very closely with the director, and is responsible for lighting each shot, choosing camera angles, lenses and filters. The lighting cameraman/woman decides how each shot should look and how best to interpret the director's intentions, but the job does not usually involve positioning or handling the camera.

Camera Operator

The camera operator handles the camera physically for the lighting cameraman/woman. The two often form a team, going from one production to the next, and their styles are closely united. The operator is responsible for a smooth and efficient camera movement, and attends to the physical details of each shot.

There will often be one or two camera assistants. The first, called the focus puller, is in charge of focusing the camera. He/

she needs a smooth collaboration with the operator. The focus puller also needs a large degree of technical knowledge.

The second assistant, called the clapper/loader, is in charge of loading and unloading the camera. He/she also fills out the camera sheets with careful records of each shot, including the type of film used, the type of lens and the number of feet of film shot. The clapper/loader also operates the clapper board before each shot.

Video camera operation in a studio is a different type of work and can require different skills. Before shooting, the camera operator will read the camera script and discuss shots and angles with the director. While shooting, the operator will wear a headset to hear directions from the director or floor manager. Excellent hand-eye coordination is needed to position the camera focus and compose the shots at exactly the right time. Outside broadcast units can mean a great deal of work away from home. You need to have a practical interest in photography, lenses and lighting and the ability to compose a shot.

Case Study
John is a *lighting cameraman.*

I started out as an assistant trainee director for the National Coal Board. Before that, I had gone to medical school for three years and had a number of jobs, including being a bus conductor. I wrote to television stations about training programmes and also to a number of large companies which, at that time, had their own film departments. The Coal Board finally wrote and asked if I was willing to be a trainee assistant director. They did a number of training and safety films about the dangers of machinery and the working conditions in the coal mines. At that time I was more interested in sound and directing, but then it hit me that I wanted to be a cameraman because of the involvement with what you are actually filming.

As other assistants began to leave or be promoted, I finally became a camera assistant. I stayed for about two years, learning as much as I possibly could; then I left the Coal Board and started doing films for local television news and current affairs programmes. During that time I travelled a lot, to Cyprus, Zimbabwe and the Middle East. I remember being shot at once, since we covered a lot of political upsets. Travel used to be one of the main attractions of the job, but after you've been to about 50 countries the novelty wears off.

My job changes from production to production. If I'm working on a documentary, there might be just myself and possibly an assistant. The assistant will do lots of things, including operating the camera and adjusting the focus. Sometimes it's just me and the camera and I get to do everything. I actually prefer that. On a commercial, I rarely even get to look through the camera. The director takes an active part and works out the shots with the camera operator. I actually set up the shot and light it, find a good position for the camera and decide on the filters. Though you do get paid more for commercials, I prefer documentaries. You have to be flexible and quick to react. There are a lot of things happening at any one time and it's up to the cameraman to react quickly and spontaneously.

There are more and more women coming into camera work. I find that women assistants are more conscientious about doing the job properly. They usually know a lot about the equipment and have great ability in handling the camera.

I have a company involving a number of camera and sound personnel. We hire trainees whenever an opening comes up, usually from film school. The students are already aware of the camera and the equipment. You also know that they love film and are serious about working in the industry.

It's sometimes hard to find work, the state of the economy being what it is. Most of mine comes from recommendations or because someone else isn't available. Some cameramen have agents, others have show reels. They take them round to companies and try and sell themselves. You need to have a lot of ambition and drive for that. Most companies tend to use the same crew over and over and you have to be quick to get in there and be in the right place at the right time. A lot of the breaks in this business are due to timing and luck.

Sound Personnel

Sound operators, recorders and mixers work in all areas of the business. In studios, they work on the studio floor setting up and operating sound booms, microphones and loudspeakers. They can also work in the control room, where they can operate the mixing desk, tape recorders and play-in machines. They are responsible for controlling sound levels and the tonal quality of the sound. On location it can range from just one sound recordist on a video tape (VT) machine to a team of boomswingers and a sound mixer to control the various sound levels.

Sound personnel rarely work both on location and in a sound studio – the two areas are very different. People working in sound should have an interest in all aspects of sound, including music, and obviously have normal hearing.

Sound Mixer

He/she is responsible for recording the sound on location and balancing the levels to make sure they are in perspective. The sound mixer usually has an assistant, the sound recordist.

Boom Handler
He/she controls the microphones which are hung out of view of
the camera. The position of the mikes is determined by the mixer
or recordist.

Dubbing Mixer
This stage of sound is in post-production in a sound studio. The
dubbing mixer supervises the recording of additional sound,
including music and some sound effects. He/she will also obtain
live effects in the studio and record dialogue that was unusable.
The dubbing mixer sits on the console and decides the
appropriate level of sound, and is responsible for post-synching,
that is, matching image to sound. The job is both highly technical
and very creative, and it often takes years of experience before
becoming a qualified dubbing mixer.

Editor
Though most of an editor's work takes place during post-
production, some minor editing may go on during shooting. A
director sometimes consults an editor to get the best possible
image from a particular shot.

The editor's job is to position the shot, choose the best angles
and frames of film and cut them together. He/she is the person
who determines the narrative structure of the film, by cutting,
editing and assembling the picture. An editor's job is incredibly
important - he/she can make or break a picture, having the
capacity to correct weak or bad shots or enhance a good one.

The editor usually has two assistants who collect the rushes
(the first prints of a film after shooting), put location sound to
picture for viewing and also join the cuts together under the
supervision of the editor. The assistants keep careful records of
each shot. Often the first assistant editor has a great deal of
autonomy and responsibility, working almost independently of
the supervising editor.

Case Study
Richard is a *commercials editor*.

> In commercials work, editors are usually working for a post-
> production or editing company. You work on whatever account the
> company has acquired. In working up to being an editor from a first
> assistant, you need to bring in clients who are willing to work with you
> to justify the increase in salary. When I was a first, I did a lot of work

on my own, and had a few people who wanted me to cut their films. When I built up a client list, I was made a full editor.

I started out working for a post-production company as a runner. At that time, I didn't know exactly what I wanted to do. In fact, I thought I might want to be a clapper/loader. All I knew was that I wanted a job that would keep me interested. And my work does.

I'm never bored with my job. It's very rewarding and very creative. Each stage is different. Because of the number of commercials I might be working on at any one time, and the different stages of editing they might be in, I do a variety of jobs in any one day. On a feature film you work on one film for months before editing is completed.

Most editors I know work for a specific company, though many well-known editors work freelance, often for the same director over and over again.

When I first started as a runner, I went all over Soho, learning about the different companies and what they were doing. I made a lot of contacts and learned about film and different techniques involved in editing. The experience for me was invaluable.

Researcher

Broadcasting researchers work as part of a production team. They can be involved in developing ideas for programmes and working on them through to completion. They need to be good at finding information and contacting people to give comments and interviews. Some have a high level of specialist knowledge in a specific subject area, others are more generalist and work on a wide range of programmes. Current affairs, documentaries and information programmes tend to use researchers the most. The feature film industry also uses researchers to check out details for historical film sets and to verify historical details for authenticity.

Studio Floor Manager

Floor managers work in television studios. They act as a link between the floor and the director to organise and coordinate all the sequences of the shoot, and also have to deal with performers and technicians to make sure they all work smoothly together. They need to be tactful, assertive, calm and confident. Many are recruited from within the industry because the jobs often require a great deal of production experience.

Job Discrimination

There are few women and even fewer ethnic minorities represented in the film and video industries. There have always been traditional 'women's' grades within the union, such as continuity and editing, but until recently there have been few camera technicians or sound personnel. This is changing slowly, mostly because of film schools and also because of the fact that much of the equipment being used now is lighter and easier to handle.

The industry has acknowledged the lack of representation of women and minorities in almost all sectors of film-making with the result that the union is now actively promoting the hiring of women and minorities, and in some cases government funding has been withheld until certain staffing quotas for a production are met. Many of the film schools actively encourage women and minorities to apply, often favouring them over the traditional white male applicants.

Ultimately there is no sure-fire way in, but sheer dogged persistence is *the* essential quality required above all others. As director and producer Tony Bulley testifies: 'The advice is always the same and that is just go at it, do it and try and try and try. There still isn't a recommended qualification or an advisable academic route in. People still come from all over. There's a craft-based side and an intellectual side, therefore even somebody with no GCSEs can come up through the cutting rooms if they get in early. You can still work a sort of apprenticeship and be paid for it. It's one of the things I really like about it. There's nothing exclusive about it and if somebody wants to get in, really wants to get in, they will – nothing will stop them.'

Chapter 3
Education and Training

On-the-job Training

There has been little formalised training in the film industry.
Traditionally, training was acquired on the job, in a haphazard
and fragmented way. You started at the bottom, as a tea boy or
messenger, and slowly worked your way up. Some still feel that
this type of training is the best, and the only, way to learn.
Although the experience is valuable, progress is slow, errors can
be passed on and the training is limited to one field.

Previously, there was more opportunity to move around
within the industry and the training received on the job by those
now established was far more extensive than the opportunities
beginners have today.

Veterans of the industry who learned on the job often have a
strong resentment towards film students. They don't want it
made too easy for those just starting out. And some people in
hiring positions have a bias against film students.

The industry is recognising the need for more training programmes and the union (see page 35) feels strongly that more
effective training and education for those entering the film
industry will increase their future job prospects.

Case Studies
Roger is a *post-production supervisor*.

> I came up through the business by starting as a runner. I worked for
> over 20 years as a cameraman, and now have my own company.
>
> When I'm looking for someone to hire as a runner, I want somebody
> young, about 16 or 17, who possibly still lives at home and doesn't
> have a lot of expenses. They don't get bored as quickly and are happy
> just running around. If they show any interest or enthusiasm, they
> can learn about the company and about editing.
>
> I don't believe film school can give any sort of experience even close

to that of working on a real film. You learn this business by working in it. The knowledge you get from film school can be gained by reading books or by making your own short films.

The film schools have little relevance to the industry. The students come out of there thinking they know it all. They want it all quickly and don't want to start at the bottom. I definitely feel on-the-job training is the best. You can't learn at school what you can by working. Sure, you can make little films and have production teams, but it doesn't prepare you for the real problems that arise. You can't substitute education for experience.

Matthew is a *production manager*.

I started really young, since I had always known I wanted to work and direct in film. I used to make movies in my spare time on rented equipment.

I wrote to a well-known director, expressing my desire to work with him and learn about the film business. I was lucky and was offered a job as a runner on his new production. At the same time, I found out I had gained a place at film school. But I decided that school wasn't the right route for me and I wanted to be involved in film-making right away. I just couldn't wait. I thought that the experience I would gain by being actively involved in a production would be more useful to me in reaching my goal.

I do feel film schools are helpful, and sometimes wonder if I should have accepted the position. It helps you learn about the various types of films, and gives you an initial, well-rounded training.

If you decide not to go to film school, you really have to love film a lot. You should make small films, study other people's work and teach yourself as much as possible about the business. You have to be determined and really strong, and you have to make sure that you are equal to competing with film school graduates for jobs.

Skillset

Skillset is the industry training organisation for broadcast, film and video. It was established to promote and develop training for the film, video and radio industries to maintain and enhance our reputation for quality skills. It is managed and funded by the BBC, Channel 4, the Producers Alliance for Cinema and Television (PACT), the International Visual Communications Association (IVCA), the Advertising and Videotape Producers Association (AFVPA) and the Federation of Entertainment Unions (FEU).

Skillset will be working with the Open University and SCOTVEC to maintain and administer NVQs and SVQs. These qualifications will mostly be earned on the job and can be obtained regardless of the way in which the person has been trained. Provided people can prove that they can perform to the required standard, they can obtain the qualification.

A training fund for freelances is also organised by Skillset to ensure that the industry has a freelancer workforce of the right size and skill level to meet its needs. In 1994 Skillset was granted about £700,000 to invest in training freelancers.

A careers pack produced by Skillset has been issued and is aimed at anyone considering entering the industry. It has been sent to all the careers offices in the UK where it has been well received. In conjunction with the British Film Institute (BFI) Skillset also has a database of short courses and courses available in further and higher education which is constantly updated. It will be a free service to individuals.

To receive your copy of the *Skillset Careers Information Pack*, write to Skillset (address on page 74) enclosing an A4 stamped, self-addressed envelope.

FT2: Film and Television Freelance Training

This used to be called Jobfit but was relaunched in 1993 with the introduction of a new trainee programme, known as New Entrant Training. FT2 trains new entrant technicians for the freelance film and television industry and organises short courses and work placements for freelancers wishing to upgrade their skills.

The New Entrant Training programme is an apprenticeship scheme, with trainees attached to various productions over a two-year training period. This is supported by specially commissioned courses at colleges and training centres. However, they do not train directors, producers or scriptwriters. The prime criteria for selection are talent and commitment but competition is intense, with up to 100 applicants for each place.

For further information, write to FT2 (address on page 74), enclosing a stamped, self-addressed envelope.

Going to Film School

A big question you might have to decide is, 'Will going to film school help me to get a job?' There is no simple answer. There are still prejudices about film students and the quality of experience gained from film studies. A degree from a film school is no guarantee of a job, no matter how extensive the education.

However, there are a number of reasons for continuing your studies at film school if you are serious about your choice of career. The competition for jobs is getting more and more fierce, and there is an increasing number of film and television studies graduates in the job market. The more knowledgeable and experienced you are, the better your chances of successfully competing for a job. Film studies will teach you about the different jobs available, give you practical experience in production and will familiarise you with new technology and equipment. It will also give you an understanding of the theory of film and communication and often a historical and critical view as well. Your tutors will be able to introduce you to members of the film industry, who may be helpful when you are looking for work.

It cannot be stressed enough that no school can guarantee employment. There simply are not enough jobs available.

Case Study
Mike is an *editor*.

> I have my own company, and often when I'm interviewing I realise how helpful film schools are. Graduates have the edge when applying for work.
>
> Depending on the school and the facilities, film studies can really be beneficial. Schools aren't perfect, but then neither is the industry. If students take advantage of the situation, they can learn a lot.
>
> On the practical side, schools give the students a chance to handle film, learn about it and understand how it works. They are usually more interested in working in film than just looking for a job. They tend to be committed and interested.
>
> A lot of people in the industry have feelings of jealousy towards film students. They came up the hard way and expect everyone to do the same. They just don't realise things have changed. The better prepared someone is to do a job, and the more they already know about it, the easier it is on me – I don't have to explain everything.
>
> The industry is notoriously anti-intellectual. Very few people take time to look at other people's work. Film schools give students an opportunity to observe and compare. They become familiar with a number of different styles of film-making. It gives them time to experiment with different ideas. When you're out in the real world, working and hustling for jobs, you don't have the time. In school you have time to think and talk and learn.
>
> Most people without any experience have to start at the bottom, as a runner for example. If you've gone to film school and possibly had

a lot of experience in one area, such as camerawork or editing, you can often skip the messenger job and become a trainee or assistant. But you have to be good. And you have to be keen. Just having a degree isn't enough. You have to love film and have used those three years in school to their best advantage.

The best film school in Britain is undoubtedly the National Film and Television School at Beaconsfield in Buckinghamshire, originally called the National Film School. Nick Broomfield, one of today's outstanding young directors, was one of its first pupils. Here he gives a picture of what it was like to be a student there, and how he was accepted in the first place.

Case Study
Nick was a *film student.*

I made my first film, *Who Cares?*, while I was still at university. I borrowed equipment from a friend who was at Cardiff University. It was an old wind-up Bolex with a zoom lens, so you got only 15 seconds of filming at a time. I had no money so I used to go round to some of the small independent outlets for film. I used to ask for 'short-ends', which was anything from 50 to 100 feet of unused film at the end of the reel. I stuck the ends together and loaded it on a spool, and that's what I shot my first film with. I didn't have to pay anything for film stock. The whole film was like that. I remember the biggest cheque I ever had to write at that time was for the lab bill. It was for £150. Now it seems nothing. My main problem was cutting it. It took a year and a half to cut, though the film was only 18 minutes long. This was because I had to work in an editing room at night after everyone had gone home. I'd come in at 8.00 pm; my whole life became 'day for night'.

When I applied to film school I realised how important it was to have made a film. It showed – I suppose – that I had initiative and was self-motivated. It let them know what I was interested in and gave the people assessing the applications something to register on. The trouble with most applications is that they are too vague, and the assessors are grappling about, wondering who the applicants are, what they are interested in, and how they'd fit in. You've got to remember that in the early days of the School there were only 25 places to be filled each year and there were thousands of applicants. The School spends four months sifting through the applications and the ones they discard at the beginning are the ones where there is nothing to back up the applicants' interests. There is nothing to evaluate them on and unless they have led a very interesting life they don't stand a chance. If you've just come out of school or university then you *must* have something to show them and to show your interest.

If you have got something to back up your application with, there is a good chance that you will get to the interview stage. There you'll find yourself in front of the heads of each of the departments – camera, script, production, direction – together with a students' representative and the head of the school. In the interview the panel will try to find out what each student is interested in. The trouble is that a lot of the applicants don't really know that themselves. They know that they are generally interested in the film industry and that they want to be in it. They have this fantasy – quite inappropriately – that they're going to have a great old time making films. It can't be stressed hard enough what a slog it is. So if you don't know what you are wanting to do, you don't stand much of a chance, since there are so many people who do.

Originally, all 25 students I was with in the founding year just wanted to make their own films. We were all producers and directors, or at least we wanted to be! Over a period of time natural divisions emerged. One of the criticisms of the early years was that it was all chiefs and no Indians. Everyone wanted to be the next Godard, and since Godard did not hump other people's equipment around, why should they?

There is some theory taught at the National Film School, but the main emphasis is on the practical side. It was highly unstructured as well, though that is changing now. There's a great deal of equipment available so people can go off and make films. Obviously, students will make lots of mistakes, but the best way to learn is by the process of error.

One of the most important aspects of the National Film School is that it gets you a union ticket. Getting into the union is one of the most daunting tasks. You can't get a job without being in the union and you can't get in the union without having a job. It's a hopeless situation at first for people who have not got a ticket from film school, and you hear terrible stories of people having to work for two years in a lab in order to get a ticket. After a while, though, you find out ways of getting in. In practice, people say, the union hurdle stops the unimaginative people from getting in, but people with imagination and motivation will always find a way.

What's really useful about film school is that it gives you three years to sort out your ideas, experiment and just find out how everything works. You learn a bit about sound mixing, a bit about editing, and so on. So when you go out into the real world of film no one can turn round and say 'this can't be done'. There is a lot of mystique built up around films, and many of the technicians somewhat resent these 'young whippersnappers' who have come out of film school and who think they know everything. So they make their jobs sound much more complicated than they actually are. But, if you have practical knowledge, you can ask reasonable things of them – and you find out that after a while they respect you for it.

There's far less prejudice against film school graduates now than there was 15 years ago. Film schools were a completely new phenomenon in the 1970s. Before that you either did a BBC training course or worked your way up through the apprentice system. So there was a feeling that these new film graduates had jumped the queue without paying their dues. And no doubt we were all slightly arrogant. Film schools were teaching new ways of making films, which were more sophisticated and efficient than those used in the industry at the time.

The other problem was that the National Film School in its early years was far less structured than it is today. In some ways this was great as it allowed us to be much more creative and to become all-rounders. Now it's much more professional and rigorous. Whether this is better or worse is something we will not know for another ten years, until the people who are now at film school start to make their own films.

Accreditation of Courses

The Broadcasting, Entertainment and Cinematography Technicians Union (BECTU; formerly the ACTT) realises that the education and training received at specific schools is equal to an apprenticeship as a messenger or runner. They feel that completion of a three-year full-time course at one of these institutions is equal to intensive practical training.

BECTU no longer credit any courses but it is hoped that Skillset, the industry training organisation, will establish an accreditation scheme in the near future.

Applying for Courses

The quality of film studies varies from school to school. Some are geared more towards the practical side of film-making and others are academic, concerned with theory and critique. If you are serious about a career in film, it is important to pick a school that provides a high degree of practical experience. You will benefit more from your schooling and your degree will enhance your employment opportunities. Choose a school that has a good selection of equipment and modern facilities, and one which encourages students to create and experiment. Some schools focus on one or two areas of film-making, such as camera work or sound. Pick one that best suits your needs.

Check out the prospectus carefully and ask about accreditation or validation of the course. Visit the centre if you can and talk to the students who are doing courses there, to get their impressions of the facilities and training on offer. Ask the course administrator what has happened to previous students since they left the course. Look over the equipment and find out how much of the course you will spend using it, and whether they will train you to operate all of the equipment which you see. Ask a few questions about the course tutors; what experience do they have of the industry? Will a work placement be part of your course? Does the centre provide funding for student productions? If so, you should be able to make a showreel which will help you to get a job when the course is over.

The competition for places is tough and you should apply as early as possible. Most schools require a sample of previous work, such as a short film, a script or photographs. There will also be a personal interview, to determine how serious a student is about film studies.

Entry requirements for courses may vary slightly but, generally, applicants must be 18 years or older and possess five GCE/GCSE passes, two of which should be at A level. Mature students (over 25) without the necessary qualifications are often favourably considered, especially if they have practical experience in film or video. You should contact the school or university concerned for specific information about application dates and entry requirements. (See Part 2 for a list of available courses.)

Chapter 4

Getting Started

Making Contacts

Your first job in the film industry may be the hardest to find. Vacancies for beginners, even those with a film studies degree, are never very numerous. And, depending on the production and economic state of the industry, vacancies may at times be almost non-existent. There are just too many people trying to get into the industry for the number of jobs available.

Only a few positions are advertised in magazines or newspapers. Most people find out about jobs through word of mouth. They hear from a friend or associate that a new production is starting, or they are recommended for a job by someone who has worked with them previously. A lot of it is luck, and being in the right place at the right time. The more people you know, the better your chances of finding employment and once you have a job you will need to keep in contact with people to let them know you are alive and kicking.

If you have been to university or have had some other form of training, the chances are that your tutors or lecturers will be involved in film and know people working in the industry who may be able to help you. There are also a number of industry organisations that have student membership. They can help to put you in touch with other film-makers, give you advice about employment, and are useful sources of information in general. They often hold lectures or seminars which give you a good opportunity to meet others in your field. When you meet someone working in film, take their name and number and ask if it would be convenient to call. Most film-makers love their work and are willing to talk to you about their jobs.

Read trade magazines and publications, making a note of new companies being formed or films starting production. Familiarise yourself with names of producers and their companies, and what kinds of movies they make. Do not be afraid to call up companies or write introductory letters, expressing your interest in working for them. They may not have a job for you, but they will remember your eagerness. You need to show that you are serious about a career in film and are determined to succeed.

Good telephone technique is an invaluable skill when making contact with companies that might employ you. You must plan out and practise what you will say. Remember to smile when you speak – the person you are talking to will hear your smile. Always keep a record of who you have phoned and when, as it can be embarrassing to call somebody up and give them the same presentation as you did only the day before.

Case Study
Linda works in *continuity*.

> To get work, you really have to keep on trying – it's a never-ending battle. With my job, I'm employed from production to production and don't work for one specific company. I'm registered with an agency that sometimes helps me to find work. Obviously, if one producer likes your work, your chances of getting another job from him are good. But there are a lot of people out there just like me looking for work, and you're always competing for jobs.

> It takes a lot of luck and perseverance. You have to work hard, meeting people and making contacts. You need to keep up to date with what's going on in the industry, what new productions are planned, and where new offices are. You need to be there first, letting them know you're available for work.

> After a while, a lot of jobs come from people who know you, more so if you're reliable and hard working. But it's tough in the beginning. Read a lot of magazines, like *Screen International*, to find out what's going on. Don't be embarrassed to call up and offer your services. Most of the people you will be talking to started that way and will appreciate your interest. Time is also an important factor. You have to get there first because there are so few jobs. The sooner you can find out about a new production, the better your chances of getting hired. You have to ferret these jobs out before everyone else.

> You'll have to be aggressive and determined. Learn not to give up and don't get discouraged. Just keep trying. In this business, if you're out of sight you're out of mind. Be active and keep yourself visible.

Applying for Jobs

'Get in any way you can,' advises Mark Samuelson of PACT, 'Get *any* job you can.' This includes messenger/runner positions and secretarial/clerical jobs. The companies involved in the film industry that you can apply to change from year to year. New ones are constantly being established. There are a number of publications with relatively up-to-date information about the various production and post-production companies. These are listed in Chapter 7.

Production and post-production companies usually have one or two messengers on their staff. They also often hire runners during production. You may need a driving licence for some of these positions. Most companies prefer someone young, about 16 or 17, and living in or around London. They do not pay very well and it is a lot of hard work. But the experience is useful and it is a foot in the door.

The openings are rarely advertised; your best chance is to write to or telephone the various companies, or appear in person, asking about jobs.

Messenger jobs can be a good beginning to your career. Most film companies will give you an opportunity to learn as much as you want, if you show interest and initiative. From a messenger, you can usually be moved up into a position of more responsibility, such as an assistant or trainee. This may take a long time, so do not accept a job thinking that within three to six months you will become an assistant. This occurrence is very rare. The messenger period is intended as an apprenticeship for you to learn more about the industry, more about film-making and how your company operates.

You may also find work as a secretary or receptionist with a production company. This leads to the possibility of moving into production work. Most companies prefer someone aged 18 or older, with good typing and shorthand skills. Some previous office experience would be helpful as a production office can be very hectic and they will want someone organised and responsible. Sometimes these jobs are advertised in local papers and there are employment agencies that deal specifically with the entertainment industry.

Many equipment hire companies employ runners or assistants. Working for one of these companies will provide a good opportunity to learn about the equipment and technology used in film-making, especially if you are interested in camera or sound work.

The film laboratories used to have extensive training schemes but, with the state of the industry at present, they have been eliminated. Most of the labs are at a constant staffing level, and there are few beginner jobs available. The labs prefer to hire someone already experienced, to avoid the long process involved in training.

If you have completed a film or television course, your chances of getting a trainee position are much improved. Most companies with a trainee position available prefer to take on someone who is partially trained and already knowledgeable about film. If you are a film school graduate and have specialised in a particular area of film, such as camera work, editing or sound, you can sometimes get a job as a third assistant or cutting room assistant. But you will have to prove that you have learned something from your schooling and that you are qualified to do the job.

Your CV and Letter

Prospecting by letter is often seen as a waste of time, but it can pay off occasionally. A great deal depends upon the letter you write, so you should plan and check it thoroughly. There are many standard types of CV and covering letter that you can copy, adapt and improve to fit your own style. To find out more about this, see *Preparing Your Own CV* by Rebecca Corfield, published by Kogan Page (1990). The presentation must be immaculate, preferably using a word processor and the best printer you can get access to. Use good quality paper and make sure you grab the reader's attention with interesting, relevant and concise information. Make your letter dynamic and powerful to hold the reader's interest and to demonstrate that you are a confident and ambitious individual.

Always try to target companies where you think you will stand the best chance of success. If you can, talk to other people who know the company you are targeting and find out what type of work they do and the sort of people they like to employ. In this way you will be able to project an image that will appeal to whoever in the company reads your letter and CV. It will also show that you have the initiative to find things out for yourself. You must be proactive; do not wait until the interview to discover that you could have told them about an aspect of your work or training that would have appealed to them.

Interviews

Preparation is the key. In order to write your letter and CV you will have done some research into what the company does. You now need to prepare for the questions they might ask you. It is worth looking at a few of the books which are available on interview technique and questions, such as *Great Answers to Tough Interview Questions*, by Martin John Yate (1992) and *Interviews Made Easy*, by Mark Parkinson (1994), both published by Kogan Page.

You are competing against people who are fanatical about what they do, so you must be highly competitive yourself. Above all, you should demonstrate that you already have knowledge of the production process and do not expect to be told everything.

Freelance Work

Until 1983, most positions within the union (Broadcasting Entertainment Cinematograph and Theatre Union) were considered freelance, or self-employed. Some jobs may last the length of the production, which in the case of commercials might be only a day or two. You will probably work in more than one area of film-making within a single year, and for a number of different companies.

In 1983 the tax laws changed and now most of these positions are considered full-time employment. You should find yourself a qualified accountant as soon as you are employed to help you with your tax. One of your associates should be able to recommend an accountant who is familiar with film and entertainment tax laws.

If you are considered by the Inland Revenue to be self-employed, you are responsible for paying your own tax and National Insurance contributions as well as being ineligible for sick pay. In other cases your employer will take care of this for you.

The union has detailed information relating to the tax status of its members, and your accountant will be able to sort out this complicated problem for you.

Part 2

Chapter 5

Courses Available

Guide to Courses

Before you undertake a course make sure you find out whether it carries some clout with people in the industry. It is also important that the course you choose is relevant to what you want to do afterwards. One way of finding these things out is to telephone or write to film companies or contact people in the industry who are specifically involved in the kind of work you are interested in. Ask them what qualifications, if any, they needed, and if they think such qualifications are necessary, or even relevant, now. A theoretical course on film in a post-industrial society can appear totally inconsequential to a producer who requires a lighting person, or, likelier still, an enthusiastic runner.

All the courses listed here are highly practical in content. There are many other film studies courses that are more theoretical. Details of these courses can be found in university and institute of higher education handbooks. They are too numerous to list here.

The subject of film studies is broadening and the courses are improving yearly. Many schools are instituting more extensive facilities and equipment. For the most up-to-date information, contact the school for specific details about courses and application requirements.

BTEC (Business and Technology Education Council), SCOTVEC (Scottish Vocational Education Council) and HND/C (Higher National Diploma/Certificate) Courses

HND/HNC courses are usually two years long and often incorporate an industrial placement. The entry requirements for these courses are usually 4 GCSEs grades A–C, a BTEC or SCOTVEC National Diploma or certificate, or their equivalent. Exceptions are made for mature students who do not have formal qualifications.

There are well over 100 colleges offering BTEC National Diploma, Higher National Diploma, GNVQ Advanced or City and Guilds courses related to the teaching of film and video production techniques. Some of the institutions are listed below but a more complete list can be found in *Media Courses UK* (1996), which costs £9.95 and is available from the British Film Institute.

The new GNVQ in Media: Communication and Production offers training within the vocational training structure and can be taken at Intermediate or Advanced Level.

Contact your local college to see if they offer one of these qualifications and ask them for course details and a prospectus. Although the courses will be similar, they may offer distinctive options and it could be worth shopping around. Some colleges, for example, will include a higher degree of practical instruction.

Barking College
Department of General Education, Dagenham Road, Romford, Essex RM7 0XU; 01708 766841
BTEC ND in Media
Two-year, full-time course with the emphasis on practical aspects of television and video production, journalism, desktop publishing and sound recording.

Basingstoke College of Technology
Worting Road, Basingstoke, Hampshire RG21 1TN; 01256 54141
BTEC ND in Media (Video Production)
A two-year, full-time course in which students will produce original and creative work in video and learn how to work as part of a team.

Bell College of Technology
Almada Street, Hamilton, Lanarkshire ML3 0JB; 01698 283100
SCOTVEC HNC and HND in Communication
The HNC course is a one-year course, the HND two years. Both are full time.

Bournemouth and Poole College of Art and Design
School of Film, Television and Audio-Visual Production, Wallisdown Road, Poole, Dorset BH12 5HH; 01202 533011
BTEC HND in Design (Film and Television Production)
This course is accredited by BECTU and recognised by BKSTS. It is a two-year course in which all areas of film and television are covered, drama and documentary being emphasised.

University of Brighton
Department of Electrical and Electronic Engineering, Cockcroft Building, Lewes Road, Brighton, East Sussex BN2 4GJ; 01273 642200
BTEC HND in Electronics for Broadcasting
A two-year course which gives a thorough grounding in electronics and applies it to the broadcast domain.

Dewsbury College
Batley School of Art and Design, Birndale Road, Batley, West Yorkshire WF13 4HQ; 01924 451649
BTEC HND in Design Communications (Audio-Visual Option)
A two-year course, covering video and audio-visual production in the publicity, information and education fields.

Dundee College of Further Education
Communication and Media Section, Constitution Road Centre, Dundee DD3 6TB; 01382 834834
SCOTVEC HND in Communication
This is a two-year course preparing students for careers in a number of the communication industries.

Farnborough College of Technology
Division of Education and Media Studies, Boundary Road, Farnborough, Hampshire GU14 6SB; 01252 515511
BTEC HND in Media Production with Business Studies
This two-year course combines the study of media production with business studies.

Glasgow College of Building and Printing
60 North Hanover Street, Glasgow G1 2BP; 0141 332 9969
SCOTVEC NC in Television Production
A one-year course providing a sound general introduction to television and video production.

Havering College of Further and Higher Education
Department of Art and Design, Ardleigh Green Road, Hornchurch, Essex RM11 2LL; 01708 455011
BTEC ND in Media
A two-year course providing a practical introduction to working in the media. Students may specialise in a variety of options in the second year.

Lowestoft College
St Peter's Street, Lowestoft, Suffolk NR32 2NB; 01502 583521
BTEC ND Diploma in Design Communications
A two-year, full-time course, giving practical experience in all aspects of the mass media.

BTEC ND in Media
A two-year, full-time course covering audio-visual production, script-writing, photography, and electronic publishing.

Newcastle College
Faculty of Music and Performing Arts, Rye Hill Campus, Scotswood Road, Newcastle on Tyne NE4 7SA; 0191 200 4218
BTEC NC and Diploma in Media
A two-year course leading to a Diploma (full-time) or to a Certificate (part-time).

North East Wales Institute of Higher Education
College of Art and Design Technology, Cartrefle, Cefn Road, Wrexham, Clwyd LL13 9NL; 01978 293467
BTEC HND in Design Communication (Film and Television Design)
Students on this two-year, full-time course have the opportunity to work in all areas of design and production.

Northbrook College
Littlehampton Road, Goring-by-Sea, Worthing, West Sussex BN12 6NU; 01903 830057
BTEC HND in Design (Audio-visual Production)
This is a two-year, full-time video production course which allows students to specialise in the second year if they choose.

Salisbury College
Southampton Road, Salisbury, Wiltshire SP1 2LW; 01722 323711
BTEC HND in Photography, Broadcast and Video Production
A two-year, full-time course. In the first year students specialise in photography or the moving image.

South East Essex College of Arts and Technology
Carnarvon Road, Southend-on-Sea, Essex SS2 6LS; 01702 220639
BTEC National Diploma in Media
A variety of units full time over two years, including film, video and television production.

South Thames College
Wandsworth Building, Wandsworth High Street, London SW18 2PP; 0181 870 2241
BTEC ND in Media
A practical and theoretical two-year, full-time course in a range of media-related skills.
BTEC HNC in Design (Television Production)
A two-year, part-time specialist TV production course covering both studio and location work.

Stevenson College
Stenhouse Street West, Edinburgh EH11 3EP; 0131 443 8888
SCOTVEC HNC in Audio-visual Technology
This course can be studied full time for one year or part time for two years.

Suffolk College of Higher and Further Education
Rope Walk, Ipswich, Suffolk IP4 1LT; 01473 255885
BTEC HND in Design (Communication)
This two-year course includes options in film and television graphics and animation.

West Herts College
Hempstead Road, Watford, Hertfordshire WD1 3EZ; 01923 257661
BTEC HND in Communication (Media Production)
This two-year course is multi-disciplinary but allows specialism in a number of different fields. It acts as the first two years of a BA (Hons) Media Production Management Degree.

Weymouth College
Department of Creative and Performing Arts, Cranford Avenue, Weymouth DT4 7LQ; 01305 208856
BTEC ND in Media
A broad foundation in media production skills and working practices. Full time over two years.

Degree Courses

The degree courses listed in this section are all highly practical. Some involve the exclusive study of film and video while others are fine art or graphic design degrees which provide the opportunity to study film and video as a major specialisation of the course. The usual entry requirements for degree courses are five GCSE/GCE passes, including two at A level. For graphic design and fine art degrees an arts foundation course is also normally required. The usual length of a degree course is three years.

The American College in London
110 Marylebone High Street, London W1M 3DB; 0171 486 1772
BA in Video Production
Four-year, full-time course offering instruction in Commercial, Documentary and Music Video making.

Bournemouth University

Department of Media Production, Poole House, Talbot Campus, Fern Barrow, Poole, Dorset BH12 5BB; 01202 595371

BA (Hons) Media Production
Students study video, computer animation and audio before specialising in one area. The course includes media law and aesthetics.

BA (Hons) in Costume for the Screen and Stage
Three-year, full-time course with Costume Design and Supervision and Costume Interpretation being the two main options.

BA (Hons) in Scriptwriting for Film and Television
Three-year, full-time, mostly practical course allowing students to learn the skills required for drama scriptwriting, documentary writing and promotional, educational and corporate programmes.

Brunel University

Department of Human Sciences, Uxbridge, Middlesex UB8 3PH; 01895 274000

BSc (Hons) in Communication and Information Studies
Practical video and computing work complement theoretical aspects of the course. Four years full time.

Canterbury Christ Church College of Higher Education

North Holmes Road, Canterbury, Kent CT1 1QU; 01227 767700

BA and BSc (Joint Hons) Combined Studies
Radio, film and TV with one other subject. Offers an opportunity to develop and practise production skills in each of the three media.

University of Central England in Birmingham

School of Communication, Perry Barr, Birmingham B42 2SU; 0121 331 5477

BA (Hons) in Media and Communication
A three-year course with specialisations in one or two media production subjects in the final year. Balances production skills and theoretical work.

University of Central London

School of Communication, 18–22 Riding House Street, London W1P 7PD; 0171 911 5000

BA (Hons) in Film, Video and Photographic Arts
This three-year course offers early specialisation in photography or film in the context of media as a means of communication.

Central Saint Martin's College of Art and Design

London Institute School of Art, 107–109 Charing Cross Road, London WC2H 0DU; 0171 753 9090

BA (Hons) Fine Art
Film and video are studied from the first year of the course.

Coventry University

School of Art and Design, Gosford Street, Coventry CV1 5RZ; 01203 838620
BA (Hons) Graphic Design; BA (Hons) Communication Studies
Students may choose to specialise in film and video on either of the degree courses.

De Montfort University

School of Arts, Degree Scheme in Arts and Humanities, Gateway House, PO Box 143, Leicester LE1 9BH; 0116 255 1551
BA (Hons) in Media Studies
Three-year, full-time course with options in film, television and video.

University of Derby

Film and Video Department, Green Lane, Derby DE1 1RX; 01332 622282
BA (Hons) Photographic Studies (Film and Video)
On the first part of the course students follow a programme of academic studies and learning practical skills, but in the second part they are expected to take considerable responsibility for their individual work programmes. The course is mainly practical.

University of East London

Faculty of Art and Design, Greengate Street, London E13 0BG; 0181 590 7722
BA (Hons) Fine Art (Time-Based Media)
Film, video and combined media are studied as a main subject along with sculpture, painting and print-making.

Edinburgh College of Art

Department of Visual Communications, School of Design and Crafts, 74 Lauriston Place, Edinburgh EH3 9DF; 0131 221 6133
BA (Hons) in Visual Communication (Film and TV)
Film and video production are studied as specialisms alongside the other subjects (photography, graphic design and illustration) of the department.

Farnborough College of Technology

Division of Education and Media Studies, Boundary Road, Farnborough, Hampshire; 01252 515511
BSc in Media Production and Technology
With students encountering the latest technologies there is equal emphasis on both theory and practice.

University of Glamorgan

School of Humanities and Social Sciences, Pontypridd, Mid Glamorgan CF37 1DL; 01443 482573
BA (Hons) in Theatre and Media Drama

Provides a range of practical and critical skills across dramatic media.

Glasgow School of Art
167 Renfrew Street, Glasgow G3 6RQ; 0141 353 4500
BA (Hons) in Graphic Design
Options include photography, animation, and film and television graphics.

Goldsmiths College, University of London
Department of Media and Communications, Lewisham Way, New Cross, London SE14 6NW; 0181 692 7171
BA in Anthropology and Communication Studies
Options include creative writing, animation and television production.
BA in Communications
Provides a sound basis for graduates entering future careers in communications and media.

University of Humberside
School of Media, George Street, Hull HU1 3BW; 01482 440550
BA (Hons) in Documentary Production
70 per cent practical and 30 per cent theory. A multi-disciplinary first year is followed by two years specialising in video photography and radio.
BA (Hons) in Media Production
BA (Hons) in Graphic Design
BA (Hons) in European Audio-Visual Production
This last course is designed for graduates who want to produce videos for the growing European market and students spend their third year in France or Spain.

Kent Institute of Art and Design
Maidstone College, Oakwood Park, Maidstone, Kent ME16 8AG; 01622 757286
BA (Hons) Communication Media: Time-Based Media Pathway
Several different pathways to work on and opportunities for original work in later stages.

King Alfred's College of Higher Education
Sparkford Road, Winchester, Hampshire SO23 4NR; 01962 841515
BA (Hons) in Drama, Theatre and Television
Emphasis is on the theory and practice of drama and documentary television.

Kingston University
School of Graphic Design, Knights Park, Kingston-upon-Thames KT1 2QJ; 0181 547 2000
BA (Hons) Graphic Design

Students on this course study animation and moving image on film and video.

University of Leeds
Institute of Communication Studies, Leeds LS2 9JT; 0113 233 5812
BA (Hons) in Broadcasting Studies
The course runs in conjunction with BBC television training. Practical, professional and academic curricula are taught in parallel.

Leeds Metropolitan University
School of Engineering, Calverley Street, Leeds LS1 3HE; 0113 283 2600
BSc (Hons) in Media Technology
Four-year course, with a two-year HND option. Students study a number of disciplines which allows them to keep their career options open.
BEng (Hons) in Electronics, Music and Media Technology
Three-year, four-year sandwich, or five-year part-time course for electronic engineers who want a career in this field.

Liverpool John Moores University
Faculty of Art and Design, Department of Graphic Design, 2a Myrtle Street, Liverpool L7 7DN; 0151 231 2121
BA (Joint Hons) Screen Studies
Combines critical understanding of film with acquisition of practical video production skills.
School of Media, Critical and Creative Arts, Dean Walters Building, St James Road, Liverpool L1 7BR; 0151 231 5052
BA (Hons) in Media Professional Studies
The course combines business and management skills with production practice.

London College of Printing and Distributive Trades
School of Media, 10 Back Hill, Clerkenwell, London EC1R 5EN; 0171 514 6500
BA (Hons) Film and Video
All stages of film and video are covered, with strong theoretical emphasis.

University of Luton
Park Square, Luton Bedfordshire LU1 3JU; 01582 34111
BA (Hons) in Media Production
A modular degree in media production giving students practical experience from which theoretical issues are brought out.

Maidstone College
Kent Institute of Art and Design, School of Visual Communication, Oakwood Park, Maidstone, Kent ME16 8AG; 01622 757286

BA (Hons) Communication Media – Time-based Studies
Time-based studies can be chosen as a specialism as part of the modular communication media degree.

Manchester Metropolitan University
Department of Communication Media, Chatham Building, Cavendish Street, Manchester M15 6BR; 0161 247 2000
BA (Hons) Interactive and Broadcast Media
This course concentrates on television production skills and interactive media design.

Napier University
Department of Photography, Film and Television, 61 Marchmont Road, Edinburgh EH9 1HS; 0131 455 2487
BA and BA (Hons) Photography, Film and Television
Students may specialise in film and television production from the middle of the second year.

University of Northumbria at Newcastle
Faculty of Art and Design, Squires Building, Sandyford Road, Newcastle on Tyne NE1 8ST; 0191 232 6002
BA (Hons) Media Production
Four areas are covered on this course: film and video production, motion graphic design, scriptwriting and media theory.

Norwich School of Art and Design
St George Street, Norwich NR3 1BB; 01603 610561
BA (Hons) in Graphic Design (Animation)
Second and third year students can specialise in the graphic and illustrative use of film and video.

Nottingham Trent University
Faculty of Art and Design, Department of Visual and Performing Arts, Burton Street, Nottingham NG1 4BU; 0115 948 6406
BA (Hons) in Fine Art
Students work with a wide range of media including 16mm film and video.

University of Plymouth
Drake Circus, Plymouth, Devon PL4 8AA; 01752 232541
BSc (Hons) in MediaLab Arts
Includes photography, video, desk-top publishing, animation, interactive multimedia and business organisation.

University of Portsmouth
School of Art, Design and Media, Lion Gate Building, Lion Terrace, Portsmouth PO1 3HF; 01705 842293

BA (Hons) in Art, Design and Media
Students take several 'pathways', each with its own distinctive character, the whole making a course that seeks to apply theoretical concepts
to practical film and video production.

Salisbury College
Southampton Road, Salisbury, Wiltshire SP1 2LW; 01722 323711
BA (Hons) in Film and Television Production
One-year course for HND students to upgrade their qualification.

University College Salford
Centre for Media, Performance and Communications, Adelphi Building,
Peru Street, Salford, Manchester M3 6EQ; 0161 834 6633
BA (Hons) in Television and Radio
The course integrates elements of production and dramatic
performance.

Sheffield Hallam University
School of Cultural Studies, Communication, Film and Media Section,
Psalter Lane, Sheffield S11 8UZ; 0115 253 2601
BA (Hons) in Media Studies; BA (Hons) in Film Studies
Practical and analytical skills are included. Students of Film Studies can
emphasise academic or practical production aspects of the course in
the third year.
BA Hons in Fine Arts
Options in film and video include practical experience of 8mm, 16mm,
Hi-8 and various other formats.

South East Essex College of Arts and Technology
Carnarvon Road, Southend-on-Sea, Essex SS2 6LS; 01702 220639
BSc (Hons) in Media Production and Technology
Four-year, part-time evening course covering a variety of media,
including video.

University of Stirling
School of Art, Department of Film and Media Studies, Stirling FK9 4LA;
01786 467520
BA (Hons) in Film and Media Studies
Theoretical and production work across a wide range of media. A four-
year, full-time course.

University of Sunderland
Forster Building, Chester Road, Sunderland SR1 3SD; 0191 515 2161
*BA (Hons) in Media Studies and BA (Hons) Photography, Video and
Digital Imaging*
Combines theoretical with practical work including video, radio, print

and photography. Students may choose the degree of emphasis put on academic and practical aspects of the course.

The Surrey Institute of Art and Design
Faculty of Arts and Media, Falkner Road, The Hart, Farnham, Surrey GU9 7DS; 01252 722441
BA (Hons) in Film and Video; BA (Hons) Animation
Provides students with a thorough grounding in all aspects of film and video production.

University of Sussex
Media Studies Faculty, Arts Building, Falmer, Brighton BN1 9QN; 01273 628019
BA (Hons) in Media Studies
Academic media studies combined with practical training in television, video and radio production.

University of Ulster
Coleraine, Co Londonderry, Northern Ireland BT52 1SA; 01265 324196
BA (Hons) in Media Studies
BA (Hons) in Visual Communication
A wide range of media is studied, including video.

University College of Ripon and York St John
Department of Drama, Film and Television, Lord Mayor's Walk, York YO3 7EX; 01904 656771
BA (Hons) in Film, Television, Literature and Theatre Studies
Practical work is central to most course units and there are opportunities to study in Europe or the USA.

University of the West of England, Bristol
Faculty of Art, Media and Design, Clanage Road, Bower Ashton, Bristol, Avon BS16 2JU; 0117 966 0222
BA (Hons) Time-based Media
Theoretical and practical work are balanced equally in this course.

University of Westminster
School of Design and Media, Harrow Campus, Watford Road, Northwick Park, Harrow, Middlesex HA1 3TP; 0171 911 5000
BA (Hons) in Contemporary Media Practice
Now part of the University of Westminster, the Harrow School of Design and Media has a long tradition of education in photography and the media. The course offers the opportunity to maintain work across a number of media.

Wirral Metropolitan College

Withens Lane, Wallasey, Wirral, Merseyside L45 7LT; 0151 639 8371
BA (Hons) in Media Studies
A modular programme which allows students to progress from a
Certificate in Higher Education, which they earn in their first year, to a
Diploma in Higher Education in their second year, to a BA Honours
Degree in their third.

Postgraduate Courses

Bournemouth and Poole College of Art and Design

School of Film, Television and Audio Visual Presentation, Wallisdown
Road, Poole, Dorset BH12 5HH; 01202 533011
Postgraduate Diploma and MA in Video Production
One-year production course with film and/or video options. Primarily
for diplomates, graduates and mid-career students.

Bournemouth University

Poole House, Fern Barrow, Poole, Dorset BH12 5BB; 01202 595371
Postgraduate Diploma/MA in Video Production
The postgraduate diploma lasts for three terms, the MA carries on for a
fourth term. This course is for graduates wishing to work as producers
and directors.

University of Bristol

Department of Drama: Theatre, Film, Television, Cantocks Close,
Woodlands Road, Bristol BS8 1UP; 0117 928 7838
Postgraduate Diploma and MA, Film and Television
This is a one-year intensive course in radio, film and television
production. Some prior knowledge of media or media aptitude is
assumed.

Canterbury Christ Church College

Department of Radio, Film and Television, North Holmes Road, Canterbury, Kent CT1 1QU; 01227 767700
MA in Media Production
This is a one-year taught course which concentrates on radio, film and
television production.

Coventry University

School of Art and Design, Gosford Street, Coventry CV1 5RZ; 01203
838534
Postgraduate Diploma and MA in Electronic Graphics
Students learn about the technology of electronic media and important

techniques such as two-dimensional graphics origination, image capture and manipulation, animation and sound.

University of Derby
Film and Video Department, Green Lane, Derby DE1 1RX; 01332 622282
MA in Film and Video
Designed for practising independent film and video makers, this course places the emphasis on the students to work through their own programme.

Duncan of Jordanstone College of Art
School of TV and Imaging, Perth Road, Dundee DD1 4HT; 01382 223261
Postgraduate Diploma in Electronic Imaging
A one-year, full-time course which leads its field in Europe. Ninety per cent of its graduates have found employment in film and television production.

Edinburgh College of Art
Lauriston Place, Edinburgh EH3 9DF; 0131 229 9311
Postgraduate Diploma/MDes Audio-visual (Film and Television)
The postgraduate course lasts for three terms, the MA for four. There is no formal, taught course.

Goldsmiths College, University of London
Department of Media and Communications, Lewisham Way, New Cross, London SE14 6NW; 0171 919 7538
MA in Television
A practical course offered in two modules; either Television Drama or Television Documentary Production.

Kent Institute of Art and Design
Maidstone College, Oakwood Park, Maidstone, Kent ME16 8AG; 01622 757286
Postgraduate Diploma and MA in Time-based Media with Electronic Imaging
Project research in time-based media with video production, sound and computer-based imaging.

Kingston University
School of Three-Dimensional Design, Knights Park, Kingston-upon-Thames, Surrey KT1 2QJ; 0181 547 2000
Postgraduate Diploma in Design for Film and Television
This is a one-year course for those whose eventual aim is to become production designers or art directors. Students are usually drawn from a number of different disciplines, including interior design, graphic design, architecture, theatre design and other communication studies.

London International Film School

24 Shelton Street, London WC2H 9HP; 0171 836 9642
Diploma in Film-Making
The School has been established for over 35 years. The diploma course lasts for two years, during which time students learn every aspect of film-making. Although most of the students have a first degree, this requirement is not strictly adhered to.

Middlesex University

Faculty of Art and Design, Cat Hill, Barnet, Hertfordshire EN4 8HT; 0181 362 5159
MA in Video
A one-year full-time course in video production for students who already have considerable experience.

National Film and Television School

Beaconsfield Studios, Station Road, Beaconsfield, Buckinghamshire HP9 1LG; 01494 671234
The school was established in 1970. It is probably the most highly regarded professionally. The three-year programme concentrates on the practical side of film-making. The school functions as a postgraduate course, although first degrees are not a requirement of admission. The average age of the students is slightly higher than usual and they may already have been employed in the film industry in some capacity. Applicants are required to submit samples of their work or to demonstrate proven ability in one or more areas of the primary instruction of the school.

Northern Media School

Sheffield Hallam University, The Workstation, 15 Paternoster Road, Sheffield S1 2BX; 0114 275 3511
Broadcast Journalism, Film and Television, Documentary, Experimental Film, Video and Audio, Film and Television Drama, and Screenwriting are all available at postgraduate Diploma level or as a Master of Arts degree
All one-year, full-time courses.

Northern School of Film and Television

Leeds Metropolitan University, Merrion Way, Leeds LS2 8BT; 0113 283 3193
Postgraduate Diploma and MA in Scriptwriting (Fiction for Film and Television)
Intensive, one-year course.
Postgraduate Diploma in Fiction Film Production
This is a one-year practical course which provides 27 students with the chance to specialise in different roles, such as direction, editing and

sound. Nine short films are made in the second term, the rights of which belong to Yorkshire Television, who part fund the production. It is also possible to spend time in Europe.

Royal College of Art

Department of Film, Kensington Gore, London SW7 2EU; 0171 584 5020
MA in Film and Television Direction; MA in Film and Television Production, MA in Design for Film and Television; MA in Animation, MA Film and Television Cinematography, MA in Film and Television Documentary, MA in Film and Television Editing, MA in Film and Television Sound
All these courses are two years long.

University of Salford

Centre for Media, Performance and Communications, Adelphi Building, Peru Street, Salford, Manchester M3 6EQ; 0161 834 6633
Postgraduate Diploma and MA in Television Features and Documentary Production
Trains the documentary makers of the future. Students specialise in one area of production. A one-year, full-time course in association with Granada Television.

Scottish Film School

Napier University, Department of Photography, Film and Television, 7 Coates Place, Edinburgh EH3 7AA; 0131 220 2972
MSc in Film and Television Production
Students entering this course already have a high level of skill and experience in either production, direction, editing, sound design or cinematography.

University of Southampton

School of Research and Graduate Studies, Highfield, Southampton SO17 1BJ; 01703 592248
Postgraduate Diploma and MA in Television for Development
The only course to offer those working in the field of development an integrated exploration of film technique and development theory.

University of Sussex

Centre for Continuing Education, Falmer, Brighton BN1 9RG; 01273 678025
Postgraduate Diploma in Dramatic Writing
For professional and aspiring writers alike, this course is supported by master classes conducted by playwrights, directors, producers and critics. Students are treated as commissioned writers from the start.

University College Warrington
Warrington Collegiate Institute, Padgate Campus, Fearnhead Lane, Fearnhead, Warrington WA2 0DB; 01925 814343
MA in Video Production
Validated by the University of Manchester, this one-year full-time course extends practical production skills and techniques in video to a professional standard.

University of Wales, College of Cardiff
Centre for Journalism Studies, Bute Building, King Edward VII Avenue, Cathays Park, Cardiff CF1 3NB; 01222 874441
Postgraduate Diploma in Film Production Studies
Students choose between documentary, screenwriting and independent production options.

Film and Video Short Courses and Workshops

The number of organisations offering short courses continues to rise every year. Although some of these courses might be useful as an introduction or, if you are already a professional, as a way to keep in touch with new technologies and practices, they are unlikely to offer the depth and breadth of training an undergraduate or postgraduate student would expect. However, it may be worth contacting some of the following to find out what services are available, especially if you are not interested in studying for one of the longer courses. If you find that none of the following organisations offer the type of course you want, the British Film Industry publication *Media Courses UK* (1996) lists another 80.

These courses and workshops offer anything from domestic to broadcast-quality video tapes, from super 8 to 35mm film and span a myriad of styles, genres and approaches. You should contact the centres directly for details of their facilities and the training offered.

Beaconsfield: National Short Course Training Programme, National Film and Television School, Beaconsfield Studios, Station Road, Beaconsfield, Buckinghamshire HP9 1LG; 01494 677903

Birmingham: Birmingham Centre for Media Arts, 21 Graham Street, Birmingham B1 3JR; 0121 233 4061

Second Sight (Birmingham) Ltd, Zair Works, 111 Bishop Street, Birmingham B5 6JL; 0121 622 5750

Brighton: Lighthouse Film and Video Ltd, Brighton Media Centre, Jew Street, Brighton BN1 1UT; 01273 202044

Bristol: Picture This, Kingsland House, Gas Lane, St Philips, Bristol BS2 0QW; 0117 972 1002

Caernarfon: Cyfle Cyf, Gronant, Penrallt Isaf, Caernarfon, Gwynedd LL55 1NW; 01286 671000

Cardiff: Chapter Filmworks Wales Ltd, The Arts Centre, Market Road, Canton, Cardiff CF5 1QE; 01222 387556

Colchester: Signals, 21 St Peter's Street, Colchester, Essex CO1 1EW; 01206 560255

Datchet: Turnip Video Services, Bishops Lodge, Oakly Green, Windsor, Berkshire SL5 4UL; 01860 370879

Dundee: Duncan of Jordanstone College of Art, School of Television and Imaging, Perth Road, Dundee DD1 4HT; 01382 23261

Dursley: Prema Arts Centre, South Street, Uley, Dursley, Gloucester GL11 5SS; 01453 860703

Edinburgh: Edinburgh Film Workshop Trust, 29 Albany Street, Edinburgh EH1 3QN; 0131 557 5242

The Edinburgh Video Training Course, 36 North West Thistle Street Lane, Edinburgh EH1 2EA; 0131 225 6518

Real Time Media Ltd, 36 North West Thistle Street Lane, Edinburgh EH1 2EA; 0131 225 6518

Video Access Centre, 25a North West Thistle Street Lane, Edinburgh EH1 2EW; 0131 220 0220

Evesham: BBC Centre for Broadcast Skills Training, Wood Norton, Evesham, Worcestershire WR11 4TF; 01386 420126

Exeter: Exeter Film and Video Resource, c/o Exeter and Devon Arts Centre, Bradninch Place, Gandy Street, Exeter EX4 3LS; 01392 219741

Falkirk: Falkirk College of Technology, Grangemouth Road, Falkirk FK2 9AD; 01324 624981

Glasgow: Glasgow Film and Video Workshop, Maryhill Community Resource Centre, 35 Avenuepark Street, Bridgeton, Glasgow G20 8TS; 0141 553 2620

Scottish Broadcast and Film Training, 4 Park Gardens, Glasgow G3 7YE; 0141 332 2201

Gravesend: London Media Workshops, 101 Kings Drive, Gravesend, Kent DA12 5BQ; 01474 564676

Hartlepool: RTV Communications, 10 Lower Church Street, Hartlepool, Cleveland TS24 7DJ; 01429 264673

Hemel Hempstead: Parallel Pictures, c/o Telecential West Herts, Unit 1A, Centro, Maxted Road, Hemel Hempstead HP2 7EF; 01442 396111

Huddersfield: Electronic Arts Video, 35 Estate Buildings, Railway Street, Huddersfield HD1 1JY; 01484 518174

Hull: Time-Based Arts, 8 Posterngate, Hull HU1 2JN; 01482 216446

Inverness-shire: The Arvon Foundation, Moniack Mhor, Teavarran, Kiltarlity, Beauly, Inverness-shire IV4 7HT; 01463 741675

Lancashire: Vision 92, 446 Burnley Road, Accrington, Lancashire BB5 6JU; 01254 394981

Leeds: Leeds Animation Workshop, 45 Bayswater Row, Leeds LS8 5LF; 0113 248 4997

Hall Place Studios, 4 Hall Place, Leeds LS9 8JD; 0113 240 5553

University of Leeds, Department of Adult Continuing Education, Leeds LS2 9JT; 0113 233 3223

Vera Productions, 30–38 Dock Street, Leeds LS10 1JF; 0113 242 8646

Leicester: Fosse Community Studios, Leicester City Council, Mantle Road, Leicester LE3 5HG; 0116 251 5577

Line Out, Fosse Neighbourhood Centre, Mantle Road, Leicester LE3 4MQ; 0116 262 1265

Lincoln: A Cutting Edge Video Access, 44–46 Monks Road, Lincoln, Lincolnshire 01522 546219

Liverpool: First Take Video, Merseyside Innovation Centre, 131 Mount Pleasant, Liverpool L3 5TF; 0151 708 5767

MITES (Moving Image Touring and Exhibition Service), Bluecoat Chambers, School Lane, Liverpool L1 3BX; 0151 707 2881

St Helens College, School of Arts, Media and Design, Brook Street, St Helens, Merseyside WA10 1PZ; 01744 33766

Women's Independent Cinema House, Blackburn House Centre for Women, Hope Street, Liverpool L1 9JB; 0151 707 0539

London: Birkbeck College, Centre for Extra-Mural Studies, University of London, 26 Russell Square, London WC1B 5DQ; 0171 631 6663

Blake College, 162 New Cavendish Street, London W1M 7FJ; 0171 636 0658

British Kinematograph Sound and Television Society, M6-M14, Victoria House, Vernon Place, London WC1B 4DF; 0171 242 8400

Connections, 241 King Street, Hammersmith, London W6 9LP; 0181 741 1766

The City University, Courses for Adults, Northampton Square, London EC1V 0HB; 0171 477 8268

Fantasy Factory Video, 175 Goswell Road, London EC1V 7HJ; 0171 608 2227

Four Corners Film Workshop, 113 Roman Road, Bethnal Green, London E2 0HU; 0181 981 4243

FX Training, 64 Weir Road, London SW19 8UG; 0181 944 0099

Island Arts Centre, Tiller Road, London E14 8PX; 0171 987 7925

Lambeth Video, Unit F7, Coldharbour Works, 245a Coldharbour Lane, London SW9 8RR; 0171 737 5903

London Film Makers Co-op, 42 Gloucester Avenue, Camden Town, London NW1 8JD; 0171 722 1728

London Screenwriters' Workshop, 84 Wardour Street, London W1V 3LF; 01932 232952

London Video Access, 5–7 Buck Street, London NW1 8ND; 0171 284 4323

Media Production Facilities, Bon Marche Building, Ferndale Road, London SW9 8EJ; 0171 737 7152

Panico Pictures, Prominent Studios, 68a Delancey Street, London NW1 7RY; 0171 284 1163

Streetlight Film Education Ltd, 21 Tower Street, Covent Garden, London WC2H 9NS; 0171 240 1575

Video Engineering and Training Ltd, Northburgh House, 10 Northburgh Street, London EC1V 0AH; 0171 490 4001

WAVES (Women's Audio-Visual Education Scheme), London Women's Centre, 4 Wild Court, London WC2B 5AU; 0171 430 1076

Luton: 33 Video, Luton Community Arts Trust, 33–35 Guildford Street, Luton, Bedfordshire LU1 2NQ; 01582 419584

Manchester: Counter Image, 3rd Floor, Fraser House, 36 Charlotte Street, Manchester M1 4FD; 0161 228 3551

Workers' Film Association, WFA Media and Cultural Centre, 9 Lucy Street, Old Trafford, Manchester M15 4BX; 0161 848 9782

Mid Glamorgan: Valley and Vale Community Arts, Blaengarw Workmen's Hall, Blaengarw Road, Blaengarw, Mid Glamorgan CF32 8AW; 01656 871911

Milton Keynes: BBC Open University Production Centre, Walton Hall, Milton Keynes MK7 6BH; 01908 655442

Newcastle: Workers' Educational Association, 51 Grainger Street, Newcastle on Tyne NE1 5JE; 0191 232 3957

Norwich: Norwich School of Art and Design, St George Street, Norwich NR3 1BB; 01603 610561

Nottingham: Intermedia, 19 Heathcote Street, Nottingham NG1 3AF; 0115 950 5434

Oxford: Oxford Film and Video Makers, The Stables, North Place, Headington, Oxford OX3 9HY; 01865 60074

Peterborough: Media Workshop, Peterborough Arts Centre, Orton Goldhay, Peterborough PE2 5JQ; 01733 237073

Poole: Bournemouth and Poole College of Art and Design, Fern Barrow, Wallisdown Road, Poole, Dorset BH12 5HH; 01202 533011

Powys: Moving Vision, Wyvern Yard, Newbridge-on-Wye, Powys LD1 6LH; 01597 860575

Reading: Real Time Video, The Arts and Media Centre, 21 South Street, Reading RG1 4QU; 01734 585627

Redhill: East Surrey College, Media Division, Gatton Point North, Claremont Road, Redhill, Surrey RH1 2JX; 01737 772611

Redruth: Cornwall Video Resource, Royal Circus Buildings, Back Lane West, Redruth, Cornwall TR15 2BT; 01209 218288

Sevenoaks: International Forum Ltd, The Oast House, Plaxtol, Sevenoaks, Kent TN15 0QG; 01732 810561

Sheffield: Sheffield Independent Film and Television Ltd, Audio Visual Enterprise Centre, 5 Brown Street, Sheffield S1 2BS; 0114 272 0304

Southampton: City Eye Ltd, 1st Floor, Northam Centre, Kent Street, Northam, Southampton SO1 1SP; 01703 634177

Sunderland: A19, 21 Foyle Street, Sunderland, SR1 1LE; 0191 565 5709

Swindon: Media Arts, Town Hall Studios, Regent Circus, Swindon SN1 1QF; 01793 493451

Wolverhampton: Light House Media Centre, Chubb Buildings, Fryer Street, Wolverhampton WV1 1HT; 01902 716044

Wrexham: Wrexham Community Video, The Place in the Park, Bellevue Road, Wrexham, Clwyd LL13 7NH; 01978 358522

York: York Film and Video Workshop, The Old Dairy Studios, 156b Haxby Road, York YO3 7JN; 01904 641394

Additional Training Opportunities

As more and more people in the film and video industry work as freelancers, training becomes more difficult, and the BBC, now that it is reducing its staff, is also reducing the number of its training schemes. The industry is therefore addressing itself to improving the training opportunities available. One of its schemes is Film and Television Freelance Training (FT2), an apprentice and freelance training system, which was originally called JOBFIT until its relaunch in 1993, now called the New Entrant Training Programme. Trainees are attached to film productions over a two-year period, and are sent to work in all the different departments: art, camera, editorial, production, sound etc. Trainees receive a monthly training allowance, and financial assistance is given for travel and child care where appropriate. At least 60 people apply for every post so applicants must expect a competitive and rigorous selection procedure.

FT2 also run two other schemes. The Setcrafts Apprenticeship Scheme is launched this year and will hope to employ six apprentices wishing to work as freelance carpenters, fibrous plasterers or scenic painters in film and commercials. Trainees will receive NVQ Level 3 Training and a salary from FT2. 4FIT is Channel 4's positive action programme for people from ethnic minority backgrounds who are new entrants to the industry and wish to become freelance assistants in the technical and production grades. As recruitment to 4FIT only takes place every two years the next intake of four trainees will not be until July 1997.

There are still about 25 places available each year. Having had some kind of job is taken as a sign of commitment and is a more effective credential than academic qualifications. FT2 can be contacted at 4th Floor, 5 Dean Street, London W1V 5RN; 0171 734 5141.

There is a prestigious two-year Theatre Studies course at the London College of Fashion which teaches costume interpretation and makeup. For more information, contact London College of Fashion, 20 John Prince's Street, London W1M 0BJ; 0171 514 7400.

A series of intensive courses is run by the National Film and Television School at Beaconsfield through the National Short Course Training Programme. These include video familiarisation (one course reserved exclusively for ethnic minorities and another reserved exclusively for women) and acting in front of the camera.

Scottish Broadcast and Film Training Limited works in Scotland to assess, monitor and provide training for the film, video and broadcast industries. Among its initiatives is the New Entrants Scheme directed at young people over the age of 17, which provides training in production and craft fields for 18 months to a maximum of eight people at any one time. Applicants must be six months unemployed and the next entry is not until May/June 1997. Contact: Scottish Broadcast and Film Training, 4 Park Gardens, Glasgow G3 7YE; 0141 332 2201.

A two-year programme of classroom-based and on-the-job training is provided to Gaelic speakers by the Gaelic Television Training Trust at Sabhal Mor Ostaig College, Skye. Trainees are given a broad grounding in techniques and practices in the television industry before specialising in a chosen area of programme-making. The course includes a one-year attachment to BBC Scotland, Grampian Television or Scottish Television, and a video production project in which students can bring together their programme-making skills. The Lews Castle, Stornoway, Isle of Lewis also offers a Gaelic Television Diploma. Phone 01851 703311 for details.

Cyfle Cyf is an organisation which promotes Welsh speakers (including advanced Welsh learners) in the Welsh film and television industry. Cyfle runs a two-year course which allows a great deal of learning on the job. Applicants must have Welsh language skills, be over 20 years old and have proven practical or theoretical experience in the field in which they want to be trained. Contact: Cyfle Cyf, Gronant, Penrallt Isaf, Caernarfon, Gwynedd LL55 1NW; 01286 671000.

In the past both the BBC and the ITV companies ran training schemes. These have been severely curtailed recently, although some are still running. It is still worth applying although competition for places is even more intense than previously.

Chapter 6

Opportunities Abroad

Job opportunities may be limited in Britain, but beware of thinking that the grass is greener on the other side. It is still equally parched. Often it is harder to get jobs abroad, since you are not operating in your own environment, and the whole process of building up contacts – essential in the film industry – is that much more difficult. The only real justification in looking for work abroad is that you want to live abroad. Then the best thing you can do is go abroad and start from there. To some people, particularly the adventurous, the challenge of living and working abroad is attractive. For them, here is a brief guide to opportunities in the English-speaking world.

United States

The USA is the capital of the world's film industry, with more film schools than anywhere else, and over 35,000 film and television graduates entering the market every year. The Penguin *Complete Guide to American Film Schools and Cinema and Television Courses* gives listings of all US and Canadian film schools, but write to the individual colleges for details of what they specialise in before committing yourself; they not only provide a variety of theoretical and practical training, but will give you your first 'wave' of contacts, essential for starting off on your career. So make sure that the school you apply to gives you not only the training you want, but also the right geographical location for what you want to specialise in. If you want to go into feature films, for example, go to a school in southern California, so you'll be in the right place to start off on your career. The following selection of some of the best schools gives some idea of the variety of courses being offered.

School of Public Communication, Boston University offers

courses in broadcasting and film, with training in screen-writing, direction, animation, TV production and multi-media presentation.

New York University offers graduate and undergraduate courses in film-making and also has a summer school in which veteran film-makers teach general film-making, sound editing, lighting and screen-writing courses.

Columbia College Chicago specialises in production courses for film, television, radio and advertising, as well as courses in animation, script-writing, editing and sound. These are all of a practical rather than a theoretical nature.

The University of Texas, Austin, has an introductory course in image and sound, and advanced courses in directing, cinematography, sound editing, film editing and video. Its most interesting course is the technical one in electronics in the media, which covers system designs, instrumentation and 'troubleshooting'. Considering that the technical and electronic aspects of film-making are the least over-subscribed, and offer some of the best job opportunities, it is probably one of the most worthwhile courses for British students to consider.

The University of California, Los Angeles, has the largest film school in the world, with courses in production, acting, cinematography, sound recording, editing, writing, animation and directing, as well as a summer school in television studies.

The University of Southern California concentrates on practical studies, with all students making their own films. The fact that graduates' films are often nominated for an Academy Award gives some idea of the high standards of the college. There are courses in production design, script analysis, laboratory work, animation and special effects. The University of Southern California also has a six-week summer school with students spending 40 per cent of their time at Universal Studios, Hollywood.

One of the most attractive aspects of film schools in the States is the large number of summer schools and workshops available, which many foreign students are able to combine with a US vacation. The American Film Institute runs a series of workshops in the summer vacation at Boston, Chicago, Dallas, Los Angeles, New York, San Francisco and Washington. Kodak also runs workshops at Atlanta, Chicago, Dallas, Hollywood, New York, Rochester and San Francisco. For more information on workshops see *The Complete Guide to American Film Schools and Cinema and Television Courses*, compiled by Ernest Pintoff, published by Penguin.

One way to find work in the US, once you have gone to live there and established contacts, is through the cable and satellite community TV stations which have mushroomed. But the main hurdle to working in the States, as in Britain, is the unions. It is impossible, however, to detail specific ways of gaining entry. Union agreements vary from state to state and from film studio to film studio, and there is no one union that dominates all others.

Canada

The Canadian film industry is dominated by the National Film Board (NFB) of Canada, set up by John Grierson in 1939 'to initiate and promote the production and distribution of films in the national interest ... and in particular ... to interpret Canada to Canadians and other countries', which employs over 1,000 people. Originally, the films sponsored by the National Film Board of Canada were documentaries, which was inevitable given Grierson's guiding spirit. In recent years, though, the NFB has sponsored an increasing number of features, among them Claude Jutra's *Mon Oncle Antoine* in 1972, which some consider to be Canada's finest film.

In spite of the work of the NFB, the US still dominates the Canadian film industry. It was to offset this that the Canadian government legislated for a 100 per cent capital cost allowance to encourage Canadians to invest in Canadian films. But any jobs that materialise from this legislation will mostly be taken up by Canadians themselves. Virtually all NFB employees and film-makers sponsored by the NFB are Canadian. In short, jobs in the Canadian film industry are hard to find, but for those who are determined enough to look for them, they are there, though hidden, particularly in the growing cable and pay TV industry. Those interested in Canadian film schools should consult the Penguin guide mentioned above.

Australia

The 1970s saw a flowering of the Australian film industry. Between 1970 and 1980, 120 Australian feature films were made with some, like *Picnic at Hanging Rock* (1977) and *My Brilliant Career* (1979), being financial as well as critical successes.

As far as jobs go, feature film-making is the hardest to break into. There are far more opportunities in the hundreds of small films and documentaries made by production companies. One of the conventional ways into the film industry is now closed in Australia; since 1960, all Australian commercials have to be shot by Australian crews.

Australia does have the first-rate Australian Film and Television School near Sydney, established in 1973, with three-year courses in directing, production, camera work, sound recording and editing. Applicants do not have to be Australian nationals, but they must be residents at the time of application. The school also has open programmes for those who have already had practical experience in film and television. For more details write to: The Recruitment Office, Australian Film, Radio and Television School, Box 126 PO, North Ryde, New South Wales 2113, Australia.

Chapter 7

Organisations, Unions, Production Companies and Publications

There are a number of industry organisations made up of members who are actively involved in film-making. Some are open to students, and others only to those professionally experienced in a particular field.

The organisations are great sources of information, especially for beginners. They often have newsletters and handbooks, run lectures and seminars and generally keep their members informed on the industry as a whole.

The following is a list of organisations, unions and production companies that will be helpful in reaching your goal. They are all more than willing to talk to beginners, and will usually put you in touch with one of their members who can offer advice and assistance. Contact the organisations directly for complete information about membership requirements, application fees and services provided.

Organisations

Advertising, Film and Videotape Producers Association (AFVPA)
26 Noel Street, London W1V 3RD; 0171 434 2651
An association representing producers and directors of cinema and TV commercials.

British Academy of Film and Television Arts (BAFTA)
195 Piccadilly, London W1V 0LN; 0171 734 0022
BAFTA developed from The British Film Academy (established in 1947) and The Guild of Television Producers and Directors (set up in 1953). As a non-profit-making company it aims to advance the art and technique of film and encourages research and experimentation. Its 3,000 members have all been elected by a central council because of their contribution to film and/or television.

BAFTA's facilities include the 213-seat Princess Anne Theatre and the 30-seat Run Run Shaw Theatre and there is always a very extensive programme of screenings, television previews and special evenings for members. Although this may sound rather exclusive, the Academy entertains over 100,000 people a year at conferences, seminars, product launches and other events, while undertaking a wide range of educational and training initiatives for young people.

British Film Institute (BFI)
21 Stephen Street, London W1P 2LN; 0171 255 1444
The BFI was established in 1933 to encourage the development of the art of film and television and provides a number of services. Its library is an information and study centre for film and television, with extensive resources; these include international books and periodicals, newspaper clippings and scripts. The BFI Production Board helps to finance British films; these films have included such productions as *Distant Voices, Still Lives, The Draughtsman's Contract* and *Three Steps to Heaven.*

The National Film Theatre, (run by the BFI), whose aim is to screen the best of international cinema, has frequent lectures and film series. The BFI also publishes a number of magazines and newsletters. There are several types of membership available; for more information, contact the membership secretary.

British Kinematograph, Sound and Television Society (BKSTS)
63-71 Ground Floor, Victoria House, Vernon Place, London WC1B 4DA; 0171 242 8400
The society was formed by British technicians in 1931 to keep in touch with major technological developments. It holds regular meetings where new equipment is demonstrated. It publishes a monthly journal with technical articles and reviews as well as a series of technical manuals. There are three membership grades, including student membership. You must be over 16 years of age and be employed as a trainee in film, sound or television, or be enrolled in a full-time film studies course.

British Screen Finance Limited
14-17 Wells Mews, London W1P 3FL; 0171 323 9080
Better known as British Screen, this organisation was set up by the government in 1986 following the disbanding of the National Film Finance Corporation (NFFC) the previous year. British Screen invests in British films and films coproduced with other countries. Its income is derived from an annual government grant, subscriptions from Rank, Channel 4, Cannon and Granada, and income from the past investments of British Screen and NFFC. In each year of its life British Screen has made film commitments of £4-5 million.

Directors Guild of Great Britain

15-19 Great Titchfield Street, London W1A 7FB; 0171 436 8626
The Directors Guild was established in 1982 to represent the interests of
film, television and theatre directors in Britain. You need to have a
professional directing credit for membership. It publishes an annually
updated Schedule of Rates that realistically reflects what directors
should expect to be paid. The Guild also runs training sessions for
members and increasingly also for the general public. It annually
publishes a directory of members that is distributed to producers,
broadcasters and other employers, and runs an observer scheme where
members have their work reviewed by another director.

Film and Television Freelance Training (FT2)

Fourth Floor, 5 Dean Street, London W1V 5RN; 0171 734 5141
Formerly called Jobfit. FT2 is industry funded and a national provider
of technical assistant grade training for new entrants to the film and
television industry.

Guild of British Film Editors

Travair, Spurland End Road, Great Kingshill, High Wycombe, Buckinghamshire HP15 6HY; 01494 712313
The Guild is a professional organisation whose aim is to see that film
and sound editing are recognised as a creative and important part of
film production. Membership is open to editors with either five feature
film credits or five years' consecutive employment in cutting rooms. It
provides seminars and workshops for members on subjects such as the
use of new technology, laboratory processes and use of video.

Skillset

124 Horseferry Road, London SW1P 2TX; 0171 306 8585
Skillset is an umbrella organisation which speaks authoritatively on
training on behalf of the independent and freelance sector of the film,
television and video and radio industries. It collects information on
existing training provision, defines the training needs of the industry,
and promotes adequate training provision for new entrants and the in-
service development of expert skills. It also promotes, monitors and
reviews equal opportunities in training provisions at all levels.

International Visual Communications Association (IVCA)

Bolsover House, 5-6 Clipstone Street, London W1P 8LD; 0171 580 0962
IVCA is a non-profit-making association representing the interests of
the users and suppliers of visual communications. It pursues the
interests of the producers, commissioners and manufacturers involved
in the non-broadcast film and video market and those of the independent facilities industry. It offers information and advice services,

publications, special interest groups, insurance and other membership services, and a monthly magazine. It also organises the UK's Film and Video Communications Festival and the IVCA Convention, a three-day residential conference, which is both a business forum and an updating opportunity.

Producers Alliance for Cinema and Television (PACT)
Gordon House, Greencoat Place, London SW1P 1PH; 0171 233 6000
PACT was formed in 1991 by the amalgamation of The Producers Association (TPA) and the Independent Programme Producers Association (IPPA). It is the trade association for British feature-film and television producers, promoting and protecting the commercial interests of producers whose primary business is the creation of television programmes and feature films. Its services include: an industrial relations service, an information service, specialist publications, a business affairs advisory service, production advice, and representation at overseas markets and festivals. It also works to ensure that the government's 25 per cent independent production quota by the BBC and ITV is implemented. Applicants for membership of PACT fall into two categories: those eligible for full membership and those eligible for affiliate membership. Affiliate membership costs £100 per year and is most appropriate for those hoping to enter the industry.

Unions

Broadcasting Entertainment Cinematograph and Theatre Union (BECTU)
111 Wardour Street, London W1V 4AY; 0171 437 8506
BECTU was formed in 1991 by the amalgamation of the two largest film and video unions, the ACTT (Association of Cinematograph, Television and Allied Technicians) and BETA (Broadcasting and Entertainment Trades Alliance). BECTU represents the interests of people employed in most technical and production jobs in film. It lobbies on behalf of the film industry and negotiates trade agreements on behalf of its members.

BECTU has recently undergone a number of changes. Because you no longer need a BECTU ticket to work in the industry, indeed only 50 per cent of those who do belong to the Union, it is offering a number of additional incentives for new members. BECTU still offers all the highly regarded functions it has done in the past but students can now join the Link Up scheme which allows access to the Union's considerable resources while studying. For £10 a year students receive BECTU's monthly journal, *Stage, Screen and Radio*, access to useful industry information and a number of useful contacts. Once you've left college you can join the Graduate Membership scheme which allows access to full Union services at a discounted rate. The discounted rate, currently

£25 a year, applies only to your first year of membership, at which point, if you wish to continue being a member, the subscription rate is 1 per cent of earnings.

BECTU claims to offer 100 services to its members, a list too long to repeat here. They include a weekly employment register, legal services and a benevolent fund. The BECTU 100 leaflet, along with Student Link Up and Graduate Membership leaflets can all be obtained directly from the Union at the address above.

Amalgamated Engineering and Electrical Union

Hayes Court, West Common Road, Bromley BR2 7AU; 0181 462 7755
This is a large, multi-industry union, with approximately 1,500 members involved in film and TV production.

Federation of Entertainment Unions (FEU)

79 Redhill Wood, New Ash Green, Longfield, Kent DA3 8QP; 01474 874606
FEU is a collective body providing coordination, liaison and representation for BECTU, FAA, the Musicians' Union, the Writers' Guild and the National Union of Journalists.

Film Artistes Association (FAA)

111 Wardour Street, London W1V 4AY; 0171 437 8506
The FAA represents extras, doubles and stand-ins and is now part of BECTU.

Production Companies

'Right now it's only a notion, but I think I can get money to make it into a concept', says the man at the Hollywood party in *Annie Hall*, 'and later turn it into an idea.' You cannot make a film without a concept, you cannot turn an idea into film without money, and you cannot get money without a production company. Production companies have other benefits to offer as well. Whether or not you have been to film school, a production company will often give you your first job. It may be a very menial job but it is a job in the film industry all the same, and will help you to build contacts for better things in the future. It is impossible to list all the production companies in Britain, but here are just a few of the larger and more dynamic ones. Some of them raise their own money for productions, others go into co-productions (often with Channel 4), while others receive backing from distributors and subsidiaries.

Acacia Productions
80 Weston Park, London N8 9TB; 0181 341 9392
Produces documentaries.

BFI Production
29–35 Rathbone Street, London W1P 1AG; 0171 636 5587
Produces, develops, finances and co-finances films. Gave Lindsay Anderson, Ken Russell and John Schlesinger the chance to make their first films. Backed *Caravaggio* (1986), *The Draughtsman's Contract* (1984) and *Loaded* (1994).

Cinema Verity Ltd
The Mill House, Millers Way, 1a Shepherds Bush Road, London W6 7NA; 0181 749 8485
Produced *Evil Angels* (1987), starring Meryl Streep, and, among other series, *GBH* (1992) and *Class Act* (1994).

Columbia Tristar
19 Wells Street, London W1P 4DH; 0171 580 2090

The Comic Strip
5 Soho Square, London W1V 5DE; 0171 439 9509

Goldcrest Films and Television
65 Dean Street, London W1V 6PL; 0171 437 8696
Major feature-film producers. Films include *The Mission* (1986), *A Room With a View* (1985) and *The Killing Fields* (1984).

Handmade Films
15 Golden Square, London W1R 3AG; 0171 434 3132
Backed by George Harrison. Produced *A Private Function* (1987), *Mona Lisa* (1986) and *Withnail and I* (1988).

Medialab
1 Margaret Street, London W1N 7LG; 0171 436 2050
Produces pop promos.

Merchant Ivory Productions
46 Lexington Street, London W1R 3LH; 0171 437 1200
Producer Ismail Merchant and director James Ivory. Made *Maurice* (1987), *Howard's End* (1992) and *The Remains of the Day* (1993).

Mersham Productions Ltd
Newhouse, Ashford, Kent TN25 6NQ; 01233 503636
Coproduced *A Passage to India* (1985) and *Little Dorrit* (1986).

National Video Corporation
The Forum, 74 Camden Street, London NW1 0JL; 0171 388 3833
Produces live opera and ballet recordings.

Paramount Pictures
UIP House, 45 Beadon Road, London W6 0EG; 0181 741 9041

Polygram Music Video
247-353 Chiswick High Road, London W4 4HS; 0181 994 9199
Makes music programmes for video release.

Prominent Studios
68A Delancey Street, London NW1 7RY; 0171 284 0242
Film production facility.

The Recorded Picture Co
24 Hanway Street, London W1P 9DD; 0171 636 2251
Produced *Merry Christmas Mr Lawrence* (1983), *The Last Emperor* (1987), *The Sheltering Sky* (1991) and *The Naked Lunch* (1992).

Scimitar Films
6-8 Sackville Street, London W1X 1DD; 0171 603 7272
Produced *Death Wish III* (1985), *Chorus of Disapproval* (1988) and *Dirty Weekend* (1993).

Twentieth Century-Fox Productions Ltd
31 Soho Square, London W1V 6AP; 0171 437 7766
A big US major, which made *Alien* (1979) and *Star Wars* (1977), and also cofinanced *Chariots of Fire* and *The Final Conflict* (with Allied Stars).

Working Title
Oxford House, 76 Oxford Street, London W1N 9FD; 0171 307 3000
Credits include *My Beautiful Launderette* (1986), *Wish You Were Here* (1987) and *Four Weddings and A Funeral* (1994).

Zenith Productions
43 Dorset Street, London W1H 4AB; 0171 224 2440
Film and TV subsidiary of Carlton Communications.

Women's Organisations

In addition to the unions there are a number of women's organisations and pressure groups whose aim is specifically to promote women in the industry and to combat any discrimination against them.

Cambridge Women's Resource Centre
Hooper Street, Cambridge CB1 2NZ; 01223 321148

Leeds Animation Workshop
45 Bayswater Row, Leeds LS8 5LF; 0113 248 4997

Second Sight
Zair Works, 111 Bishop Street, Birmingham B5 6JL; 0121 622 4223

WHEEL (Women's Health, Education, Entertainment and Leisure)
Wesley House, 4 Wild Court, off Kingsway, London WC2B 4AU; 0171 831 6946

Women's Independent Cinema House (WITCH)
Blackburn House Centre for Women, Hope Street, Liverpool L1 9JB; 0151 707 0539

Women in Film and Television, Garden Studios, 11-15 Betterton Street, London WC2H 9BP; 0171 379 0344. Full members must have three years' professional experience.

Women's Media Resource Project
89a Kingsland High Street, Dalston, London E8 2PB; 0171 254 6536

Publications

Following is a selection of film and television publications including journals, magazines, newspapers, updates and books. Many can be obtained directly from the organisation involved, or purchased from specialist film bookstores or newsagents around Soho in London. A number can also be studied in the BFI library. A few of the publications have job advertisements.

Journals
Broadcast: 33-39 Bowling Green Lane, London EC1R 0DA; 0171 837 1212
Specialises in television and radio industry news and developments, including satellite, cable and video. Published weekly.

Film Review: 9 Blades Court, Deodar Road, London SW15 2NU; 0181 875 1520
Publishes information about all English language films on release and in production. Published monthly, with four quarterly specials.

Stage, Screen and Radio: BECTU, 111 Wardour Street, London W1V 4AY; 0171 437 8506
House journal for BECTU members. Published ten times each year.

Framework: Sankofa Film and Video, Unit K, 32–34 Gordon House Road, London NW5 1LP; 0171 485 0848
Very intellectual magazine on film theory and aesthetics. Published occasionally.

IVCA Update: IVCA, Bolsover House, 5–6 Clipstone Street, London W1P 8LD; 0171 580 0962
A monthly update for IVCA members.

Pact Magazine: PACT, Gordon House, Greencoat Place, London SW1P 1PM; 0171 233 6000
The magazine for members of the Producers Alliance for Cinema and Television (PACT).

Screen Digest: 37 Gower Street, London WC1E 6HH; 0171 580 2842

Screen International: EMAP Business Communications, 33–39 Bowling Green Lane, London EC1R 0DA; 0171 505 8000
Cinema industry magazine with news of productions. Published weekly.

Sight and Sound: British Film Institute, 21 Stephen Street, London W1P 1PL; 0171 255 1444
International critical journal. Most established film magazine in Britain. Published monthly.

The Stage: 47 Bermondsey Street, London SE1 3XT; 0171 403 1818
Independent weekly trade paper covering all aspects of the entertainment industry.

Television: Royal Television Society, Holborn Hall, 100 Gray's Inn Road, London WC1X 8AL; 0171 430 1000
Royal Television Society (RTS) bulletin with events and television industry news items. Since the arrival of Channel 4 it contains articles and news on the film industry, particularly where there is a film production company co-production with Channel 4.

Televisual: St Giles House, 50 Poland Street, London W1V 4HX; 0171 439 4222 Published by Centaur Communications Limited, *Televisual* is the monthly magazine for independent producers seeking business news about all areas of the television industry.

Books and Reference Books

Most of these are available at the BFI Library, entrance to which is £7.00 (concessions £3.00) per day for non-BFI members. Westminster Reference Library in London also has a well-stocked section of books on the media.

The Complete Guide to College Courses in Film and Television: Penguin, 1992
Gives full listings of film schools and workshops in the USA and Canada.

BFI Film and Television Handbook: British Film Institute
Annual. Contains excellent listings of colleges, workshops, organisations, hire facilities and production companies, as well as good end-of-year articles on the state of British films.

Broadcast Production Guide: International Thomson
A directory of virtually all the companies involved in film and broadcasting in Britain.

Careers in Television and Radio: Michael Selby, Kogan Page, 1996

Corporate Video Directing: Howard Hall, Focal Press, 1993

Directory of International Film and Video Festivals: British Council, 1988
Films, television and video festivals. Contact addresses and criteria for awards.

Fade In: The Screenwriting Process: by Robert Berman, Butterworth/Focal Press, 1989

The Filmgoer's Companion: by Leslie Halliwell, Granada
The classic reference book on films. It is a biographical dictionary, with additional sections on subjects and fictitious characters.

Halliwell's Film Guide: by Leslie Halliwell, HarperCollins
Great tome, with over 10,000 entries, plus credits and critical opinions.

Lights, Camera Action! Careers in Film, Television and Video: by Josephine Langham, British Film Institute, 1993

Media Courses UK 1996: edited by Lavinia Orton, British Film Institute, 1995

The Production Assistant's Survival Guide: Kathie Fraser, BBC (nd)

Video Lighting and Special Effects: by J R Caruso, Prentice-Hall 1991

The Video Makers Handbook: by Roland Lewis, Pan Books Ltd, 1991
A comprehensive practical guide.

Job Advertisements

Jobs are advertised in the following publications:

BECTU jobs listing
Broadcast
Campaign
City Limits
The Daily Telegraph
The Guardian (Mondays and Saturdays)
The Independent (Tuesdays)
The Evening Standard (London)
The Observer
Screen International
The Stage
The Sunday Times
Televisual
Time Out

Chapter 8

A Very Short History of Film and Video

Early Days

The first motion pictures made were two-dimensional, black and white, and very short - one or two minutes at most. They were shown on a kinetoscope, developed by the American inventor Thomas Edison, in 1889. Edison opened his first public kineto-scope parlour on Broadway, New York, in April 1894. The viewer looked through a peephole into a darkened cabinet and turned a spool. The 50-foot film ran for less than a minute. The first films shown on the kinetoscope were factual: a baby being bathed, a dog with a bone, an erotic dance and a boxing match.

The basic principles of the cinema had been known for centuries. The *camera obscura* had been invented in Italy in the sixteenth century, and the magic lantern had been first des-cribed by the Jesuit, Athanasius Kircher, in 1646. What made the leap from these Renaissance toys to the cinema was the invention of photography by Fox Talbot, and the observation by Peter Mark Roget of Roget's *Thesaurus*, while looking through a Venetian blind, that movement could be broken down into a series of separate phases - both in the early nineteenth century.

At the same time that Edison was developing his kinetoscope, a Frenchman, Emile Reynaud, was working on what he called his praxinoscope, based on hand-drawn images projected on to a screen, making him the father of animation. Edison's 'peepshow' used photography but not projection. Reynaud's praxinoscope used projection but not photography. The two concepts were brought together by another Frenchman, Louis Lumière, who staged the world's first film projection at the Grand Café in Boulevard des Capucines in Paris on 28 December 1895. The following year, 1896, saw the first kiss on the screen, a 15-second extract from the popular play, *The Widow Jones*, starring Mary Irwin and John C Rice. The motion picture industry was born.

That same year saw the first public cinema showing in Britain, at the Marlborough Hall in Regent Street, London, on 20 February 1896, by yet another Frenchman, Félicien Trewey, a conjuror by profession. In June, the Prince of Wales visited the Alhambra Theatre and watched his own horse, Persimmon, win the Derby. It was the British film industry's first Royal Command Performance.

The cinema mushroomed but the films that were made remained documentaries. Motion picture cameras covered the Oxford and Cambridge Boat Race, the Boer War and Queen Victoria's funeral. With the new century, storylines and fiction films made their first appearance. In 1902 Méliés made his famous *Trip to the Moon*, the world's first science fiction film, and in 1903 Edison filmed *The Great Train Robbery*, the first Western. Inevitably, the first popular fictitious film made in Britain was about an animal, *Rescued by Rover* (1905).

George Pearson, Britain's first major film producer, described this embryo cinema in his autobiography: 'Suddenly things happened, someone turned down a gas-jet, the tin apparatus burst into a fearful clatter, and an oblong picture slapped on to the screen and began a violent dance. After a while I discerned it was a picture of a house, but a house on fire. Flames and smoke belched from the window, and the miracle of miracles, a fire-engine dashed in, someone mounted a fire escape, little human figures darted about below and then ... Bang! ... the show was over. Exactly one minute ... I had been to the cinema.'

Film-makers had always sought to add colour to film and, in the spring of 1896, hand-coloured films were exhibited. The process was tedious and time-consuming. Many different techniques were tried to add colour, including stencils, chemical toning and dyes, but none could satisfactorily reproduce the original colour. A two-colour system, the kinemacolor process, was developed in 1906 and remained popular for over ten years. The first technicolour film, *The Toll of the Sea*, was shown in 1922 and was a big step forward. By the end of the 1920s many films, including *Broadway Melody of 1929*, were in colour.

In the early 1900s most movies were still exhibited in fairgrounds and were basically one-person operations. Producers devised their own equipment, their families acted and they distributed and sold their own films. By the second decade of cinema's existence, however, there was a tremendous change.

Feature-length films which had a distinct, narrative structure were being made. An entire industry was being established around the making of movies. A hierarchy developed with producers, directors and actors having separate and clearly defined responsibilities. The cost of production increased enormously. Studios were being constructed in and around London, and Hollywood dominated the motion picture industry.

The Talkies

It took movies over 30 years to learn to speak. Edison was unsuccessful at matching sound to picture in his original machines. Most movies were shown with some sort of musical accompaniment, from a lone piano player to a full orchestra. After the turn of the century most feature films had musical scores specially composed for them. Music, however, was not the only sound that accompanied these early movies. Some cinemas were equipped with special machines that provided sound effects, ranging from the sound of horses galloping and birds singing to the sound of gunfire. The films of D W Griffith, such as *Birth of a Nation*, had elaborate musical scores which were obviously more successful in larger cinemas with proper facilities than small town movie houses.

It was clear that satisfactory sound accompaniment had to be recorded and reproduced mechanically. By the early 1920s, some of the problems were overcome. But the most pressing problem was making certain that sound and image fitted perfectly. The first systems had the sound recorded on a separate disc and then 'synched up', but to synchronise it perfectly the sound was needed on the same strip of film. Experiments proved that sound waves could be converted into electrical impulses and then registered on the celluloid itself; this would become the sound track, the narrow band running down the edge of the film and printed directly on it.

At this time large film companies were not interested in talking movies and were more concerned about the threat of radio. Warner Bros was the first big studio to take the risk with sound. They built their own sound stages and, working with Western Electric, were able to produce their own sound pictures. They were still using the sound on disc method rather than trying to fit sound on to film. *Don Juan*, starring John Barrymore and Mary Astor, was the first film premiered with a fully synchronised score. Although audiences were more interested in musical accompaniment than talking pictures, the movie was highly successful and ran for over six months. But it was *The Jazz Singer*, with Al Jolson, that assured the domination of American films in the talkie era. It premiered on 9 October 1927 and, although movies already talked and sang, something about this film captured the imagination of the audience and the rush was on. Most film companies now investigated and researched sound for film and agreed to perfect the sound on film method, rather than sound on disc which was what Warner Bros used. In 1928 nearly 80 feature length films with sound were made. The silent film was now dated and archaic. Warner Bros released the first all-talkie, *Lights of New York*, which, although not a very good film, was a huge success. Fox, MGM, Paramount, Universal and RKO all had talkies out in that year. Walt Disney also produced a talking animated cartoon in 1928, *Steamboat Willie*; it starred a mouse called Mickey.

By the end of 1928 every significant American studio had talking pictures on release. Cinema attendance had been falling and sound came at a good time. There was a renewal of interest in the movies with the addition of this novelty and box office receipts increased about 50 per cent with the introduction of sound. The film industry rode out the stock market crash of 1929 - much of this being because of the experimentation and addition of sound to picture.

Sound also changed the nature of film production drastically. New sound stages had to be built at all the studios. New technology - silent cameras, microphones on booms - had to be developed. The careers of many well-known silent film stars, such as John Gilbert, were ruined when it was found that their voices were not acceptable on film. The comedians were the hardest hit. Buster Keaton and Harry Langdon were just two of the casualties. Audiences also became more discerning. They wanted stories along with sound. Sound films survived their original novelty value and became acclaimed in their own right.

By 1933, although there was little money around, audiences still seemed to find it to go to the movies; they wanted dreams in cinemas to escape the poverty in real life. So films acquired a new dimension with sound and large-scale, lavish musicals benefited greatly. Busby Berkeley, the master of spectacle, had movies out like *42nd Street, Footlight Parade* and probably his best known, *Gold Diggers of 1933*. RKO had an unbeatable team with Fred Astaire and Ginger Rogers, who danced their way into the hearts of millions. Horror movies, such as *King Kong, Dracula* and

Frankenstein helped audiences escape from the harsh realities they faced. The 1930s was also the richest decade for comedies, as laughter was another antidote to the economic depression.

The Influence of Hollywood

The British film industry was used to growing up in the shadow of Hollywood and talkies ensured the dominance of American films. By 1929, Hollywood was turning out talkies faster than Britain could accommodate them, but by the end of 1930 all main British studios had converted to sound production. British films had broad appeal ranging from comedies to harshly realistic documentaries, but it was difficult getting them shown on home territory. The major Hollywood companies still had a lot of control in Britain. They produced films in this country for the British market, and Warner Bros even set up an American production company in Britain.

In 1927 the Cinematograph Film Act (Quota Act) was passed, which established a quota for the number of British films that had to be shown. Its aim was to ensure the distribution and exhibition of British-made features, providing a stimulus to production. Many British distributors were merely branches of major Hollywood studios and handling the home product was not a priority, just a routine. The studios scheduled their own films far in advance of release and packaged less popular American films with the more prestigious. Instead of encouraging the production of quality British films, the quota was filled by quick, cheaply made films that were rushed out.

Possibly because of the dominance of Hollywood and the artificial protectionism of the Quota Act, British film-makers made little effort to compete with American feature films. Instead, Britain developed another form of film art, the documentary. It became Britain's greatest contribution to the cinema in the inter-war years, and the parent of television realism. The guiding light behind the British documentary movement was John Grierson who, although he visited Hollywood in the 1920s and wrote perceptively about fiction films in the 1930s, was never interested in film as entertainment. He drew his inspiration from the socialist realism of Eisenstein and the romantic naturalism of Robert Flaherty. Nor were the majority of those who worked with Grierson interested in film as entertainment. They were upper middle class, Cambridge-educated, radical and idealistic. Hollywood was enemy territory.

The central figure in these documentaries - *Drifters, Man of Aran, Coalface* and *Industrial Britain* - was man, man struggling against nature, and discovering his dignity in that struggle. Thanks to Grierson the real world was opened up to the cinema. As he said, 'The raw can be finer (more real in the philosophic sense) than the acted article. Spontaneous gesture has a special value on the screen.'

But documentaries were hardly entertainment, and in the world of entertainment British films were still suburban compared to Hollywood. Already by the mid-1930s it was obvious that the quota did not create a flourishing entertainment industry. There was a migration of talent to Hollywood, which paid higher salaries, had bigger production budgets and better working conditions but, at the same time, talented European refugees were coming to Britain, adding quality to British films. During the second half of that decade, the film industry was hit by a major depression. Britain could not compete with American companies which began buying up bankrupt studios and filming in Britain. The City was not providing finance, studios were in trouble and there was a much needed injection of cash when Americans arrived to film. Twentieth Century-Fox and Henry Fonda came to Britain in 1936 and produced the first technicolour film in this country, *Wings of a Morning*. Although the backing was American, the film brought much needed work and experience in colour photography to Britain. In 1937 Robert Taylor filmed *A Yank at Oxford* for MGM which provided another injection of cash into the floundering British industry.

Then a government committee repealed the quota. By the end of the 1930s cinema attendance was booming again, mostly for the American product. Distribution and exhibition were extremely profitable, but British film production was still depressed. British films just could not compete, either here or in America. The quota was reinstated, but films now had to meet certain minimum production costs. This effectively killed off the 'quickie quota' film. Many of the films produced involved American studios at some stage and they now began serious production in Britain.

The British Film Industry

The outbreak of the Second World War almost killed the British motion picture industry. Cinemas were closed and studios were commandeered but, following pressure from the film industry, cinemas quickly reopened. Alas, the early British war films hardly justified the reopening of the cinemas, and films such as Alexander Korda's *The Lion Has Wings* were as boring as they were supposed to be uplifting. Only in documentaries did film rise to the occasion. Documentary metamorphosed itself into propaganda and propaganda metamorphosed itself into art. In the hands of Grierson and his protégés, cinema became a major weapon, with films such as Pat Jackson's *Western Approaches*, Humphrey Jennings' *Fires Were Started* and Harry Watts' *Target for Tonight*. There was nothing crude, preaching or heavy-handed about them. They were harsh and realistic, concerned less with ideas than with ordinary people, and ordinary people flocked to see them: 2¼ million went to see Crown Film Unit documentaries in 1940; by 1944 this figure had swollen to 6½ million.

The early war documentaries were made on a shoe-string. Humphrey Jennings' *Fires Were Started* used amateurs (the novelist William Sansom playing Barrett, the new fireman). They were cheaply made, hard-hitting and, in terms of ideology, highly unofficial and often disapproved of by those in authority. By the middle of the war the government's attitude had changed. Vast budgets were imposed, big-name scriptwriters like Terence Rattigan and E M Forster were conscripted and professional actors began to make their appearance. In the films that emerged – *Desert Victory*, *Tunisian Victory* and *Burma Victory* – there was a loss of quality. The ultimate of the documentary block-busters, *The True Glory*, an 'official' record of the war, which used a total of 6½ million feet of film and was narrated in pretentious blank verse, had all the pomp of an Elgar Symphony.

The early war documentaries did, however, have a profound effect on conventional British cinema – after its embarrassing start with *The Lion Has Wings*. A beginning had already been made in 1940 with the release of two British films: *Proud Valley* (the story of a negro, Paul Robeson, who moves into a Welsh mining village, is first rejected and then accepted, and dies saving the life of the son of the man who first befriended him) and *Love on the Dole* (which can be compared to George Orwell's *Down and Out in Paris and London*). As unexpected box-office successes, they showed that there was an intelligent and discerning audience hungry for more than just 'quota quickies' or melodramatic life-stories of Queen Elizabeth I. A whole genre of films merging documentary and drama – *In Which We Serve*, *The Way Ahead* and *One of Our Aircraft is Missing* – grew up. But the greatest of all war-time films had nothing to do with the war: Laurence Olivier's adaptation of Shakespeare's *Henry V*. Yet, in spite of the scope and the relevance of these films, the standard comedies of Will Hay and George Formby probably did more to keep up British spirits than all the Griersons, Robesons and Oliviers put together.

With the end of the Second World War, the new cinema talents who had emerged in the war years collected at Ealing Studios. There they produced a series of great British comedies – *Passport to Pimlico, Hue and Cry, Kind Hearts and Coronets, Whisky Galore* and *The Titfield Thunderbolt*. They combined comedy and realism, the banal and the ridiculous.

Ealing had fully equipped studios by 1931 and had been set up by Basil Dean. The company was known as Associated Talking Pictures. Dean was the first theatrical personality to promote talking pictures and he tried to encourage other theatrical staff to make the move to the new medium. Directors Carol Reed and Basil Deardon were just two he convinced. In 1938 – the company was then called Ealing – Michael Balcon replaced Dean as the head of production. Balcon prided himself on the family atmosphere but, as Harry Watts who worked there has pointed out, there were three separate hierarchical dining rooms.

There was a considerable difference in the atmosphere at Ealing and the attitude at major American studios. During the 1930s and 1940s, production in America was dominated by a handful of studios. They were involved in production, international distribution and theatre ownership. They had entire stables of talent, from actors and directors down to their own police and medical teams. They looked after their own but expected complete devotion and loyalty in return. They told their players how to act, dress and perform. Although the studios encouraged high standards, many in the stable wanted to break out on their own. Actors and directors wanted to work independently, and with the threat of television looming, it was cheaper for studios to have fewer employees on contract full time. The studio system began to fall apart. They let many people go, closed some of the stages and also began financing and distributing independent films.

Ealing Studios were sold to the BBC in 1955. Production continued at MGM's Borehamwood Studios and Ealing made its final film in 1959.

The death of Ealing was a sign of the times. Already, by the late 1940s, J Arthur Rank and Hollywood so dominated the British cinema industry that they had a virtual monopoly. A Board of Trade Report – *Tendencies to Monopoly in the Cinematograph Film Industry* – recommended the nurturing of independent companies as a safeguard against the power of Rank and the Americans. American films were heavily taxed, but rather than safeguard British films it simply provoked the Americans into retaliating with a boycott, while post-war Britain lacked the risk capital to build an independent industry. So pessimistic was the film industry that the main union, ACTT, even advocated nationalisation and the President of the Board of Trade, Harold Wilson, told Parliament: 'Apart from Rank, pretty well the whole of the rest of the industry is now facing a stoppage unless financial provision is made available.'

What saved British films was Harold Wilson's National Film Finance Corporation, set up in 1948 with a government loan of £5 million, and boosted in 1950 with the 'Eady Levy' (named after Sir Wilfred Eady of the Treasury) of a small sum on every ticket sold, to provide finance for British film productions. It came just in time. For a new threat to the cinema was appearing: television. In 1950, when there were only 400,000 television licences, 1,396 million cinema tickets were sold in 4,483 cinemas. By 1970, when there were 16 million television licences, only 200 million admissions were made in 1,558 cinemas.

The film industry immediately saw television as the enemy, and threatened to boycott any producer who sold his film rights to television. They need not have worried. For television proved a liberation for films, widening the horizons of the cinema, giving the film new dimensions and replacing the captive audience with a discerning one. Rank was the first of the cinema barons to see this and bought up interests in Southern Television, quickly followed by Bernstein's Granada, thus beginning a process that has continued to today, even going into reverse, with Channel 4 becoming one of the main sources of finance for feature films in Britain.

The cinema industry, unable to peer into the future, fought television with family fare and 'cheapies'. Hammer horrors, *Carry On* comedies and complacent war films became the order of the day. The cinema continued its decline until the early 1960s when a 'new wave' of creativity burst on to the screen. *Room At The Top* with Laurence Harvey signalled this change. Profound social and cultural changes had taken place in Britain; it was a time of protest and demonstrations, with the Suez 'moment

of truth', anti-nuclear marches and a new affluence and consciousness among teenagers.

At the National Film Theatre, new independent film-makers were showing their work in documentaries. Most dealt with other young, working class people. The film-makers were trying to put a more personal view into film documentaries and rejected studio sets in favour of location shooting, preferably in industrial cities using black and white film and natural lighting. The films were based on books and plays by authors with experience of working class life in the provinces: those who produced *A Taste of Honey*, *The Loneliness of the Long Distance Runner* and *Saturday Night and Sunday Morning* among others.

In 1963 Lindsay Anderson, one of Britain's New Wave, released his first feature film, *This Sporting Life*. In that year over a third of the films generally released dealt with aspects of contemporary life in Britain. But, also in that year, *Tom Jones*, financed by the American studio, United Artists, was a huge success. The theme of the movie, being uninhibited and free spirited, caught the mood of the moment. London was swinging and America was ready to cash in. James Bond also made his first appearance then. He was cool, knowing and stylish – characteristics of the 1960s. Britain was by then the music and fashion capital of the world; being British was 'in' and American companies were more than willing to capitalise on this. Many of the New Wave film-makers made features during this period; *Darling*, *Morgan* and *Alfie* showed London life at its best (or worst). American companies realised that production costs were lower in Britain and there was a great wealth of untapped talent available.

Many of the same changes sweeping Britain were also affecting America during the 1960s. It was a time of social change and revolution, with the new Kennedy administration, the political and social awakening of blacks and women, and the war in Vietnam. Television was also rising in importance and Hollywood began to experiment with new techniques to stem the tide. Many of the key figures of the golden age of Hollywood died or retired and major studios were less and less successful. *Bonnie and Clyde* and *The Graduate* confirmed the birth of a new era. The stars and directors of these new movies were training in New York theatre rather than Hollywood sound stages. Television replaced Broadway or studio-trained talent as the fund of writers and directors. Television was a medium offering excitement to talented creative young people, especially in that time of dwindling box office receipts and rising production costs.

By the end of the 1960s it was obvious that cinema success depended on the appeal to younger filmgoers, those with the time, money and energy to go to movies; they formed the bulk of the cinema audiences. Although the new generation may have rejected the dreams and myths of the old Hollywood, there were new dreams to replace them, signified by the success of small, intimate movies such as *Easy Rider* and *The Wild Bunch*. By the end of 1968 almost 90 per cent of British features were American-financed. The native industry was all but dead. By 1969, however, most Hollywood film companies were heavily in debt and 'Britishness' was *passé*. The British New Wave, long dead, and the success of American-financed British films signalled the change. British cinema had lost most of its native character and became part of the transatlantic movie culture.

It survived on the strength of a few outstanding directors who had come up through the 1960s' New Wave. Few of these directors had gone through the conventional studio system. John Schlesinger, Richard Lester, Ken Russell, Ken Loach and Peter Watkins came up through television. Nicholas Roeg, Hugh Hudson, Ridley Scott and Alan Parker came up through advertising. Some of the films they made, like the films of Garnett and Watkins, were super-realist, others like Roeg's *The Man Who Fell To Earth* had all the slickness of a toothpaste advert, and a few, like Ken Russell's films, were just plain bizarre. What they all had in common was that they appealed to minority audiences which, pre-Channel 4, television either could not, or would not, reach. Cinema was no longer a victim of television. It had become an alternative to television.

While cinema in the 1970s was directing itself at minority groups (mostly one group – the young educated middle class who could afford the price of the ticket), Britain's first National Film School was growing up at Beaconsfield in Buckinghamshire. By the mid-1970s the first students to graduate from there – though there were only 25 each year in the early years – were making their first small features and documentaries: Nick Broomfield and Joan Churchill's *Juvenile Liaison*, Michael Radford's *The White Bird Passes*, Roger Christian's *Black Angel* and Jana Bokova's documentary on Don McCullin. In the 1980s, they reached their maturity.

With this film renaissance came a new technical excellence, which resulted in many American productions, such as *Star Wars*, *Superman III* and the James Bond films, using British studios and cutting rooms for their technical effects. The seeds of this technical excellence can be found in the industry's grounding in advertising and in what director Ridley Scott (who made *Alien*) calls '30-second feature films'.

The greatest boost for the young film-makers was the arrival of Channel 4. Rather than steal from the cinema the minority market that the cinema had cultivated, it provided finance for new productions and gave producers a new type of deal in which films had six months at the box office before being shown on the screen. As producer David Puttnam put it: 'If a film does well there is a prospect of financial benefits. At the very worst the cost of the cinema exposure can be written off as valuable advance promotion for the film's appearance on TV or its sale to international markets.'

Since its creation Channel 4 has pumped £40 million into British films. This created a new relationship between film and television. David Puttnam described the result as 'a period of renewal in British film production without parallel in the film industry's chequered 70-year-old history'. These films were generally low budget; *My Beautiful Launderette* cost £650,000. They signposted an entirely new method of film financing which was imitated by the ITV companies and the BBC which began making films for box-office release.

The deregulation of television and the single European market have linked even more closely the fortunes of film and TV. As a result of this blurring of the divisions between the two, workers in the industry have had to become more versatile, being prepared to work in a number of the different sectors of the industry. The opportunities for working on feature films are still limited, with only 20 to 30 being made in Britain each year. In recent years, the BBC has also reduced the number of its employees from 28,000 to 22,000 and the independent television companies from 16,000 to 12,000. New entrants to the industry should look more closely to the area of the industry which has grown most rapidly in the last few years: the video sector.

Video

One of the reasons for the reduction of the number of employees by the broadcasting companies is that they are now obliged to commission 25 per cent of their programmes from independent producers. This has obviously had a beneficial effect upon independent production companies. Companies who previously only produced for commerce and education are now moving into film and television production.

With the growth of cable and satellite channels, demand for broadcast films has further increased. One of these satellite channels is MTV Europe. Its programming consists almost entirely of pop music videos, pop star interviews and rock concerts. It reaches 61.8 million homes in 37 European countries, having grown enormously since it was launched in October 1988, when its audience was 3.5 million in ten countries.

The growth of MTV Europe highlights the increased demand for music promo videos. These are made by independent companies which are commissioned by record companies to promote their acts. Budgets and production standards vary enormously. They use every 'state of the art' production device available to them. Many of the people who work on pop videos are very young. Editors really come into their own with pop videos and they are as important as the director and camerapersons.

The companies that produce music promo videos often also produce videos for commerce and education. There are many successful film and video companies that make high-quality, imaginative films for clients. The client may be a local authority, a record company or a multinational corporation. These videos must satisfy three audiences: the commissioning client, the company using the video and the viewer. It is now recognised that any subject can be visual if it is approached imaginatively. Standards have to be high because the product will be viewed repeatedly and competition is fierce.

This sector is far more accessible to newcomers than the feature film sector. It is a sector which needs new people and ideas and is a recommended route for people trying to get into film and video. Lol Creme of Medialab, one of the biggest producers of 'promo' videos in the UK, affirms: 'I think the video revolution, where equipment used for filming is light and portable, and where you don't need huge crews, has made it possible to break into the film business.' A considerable number of the personnel who work on such productions also work in the established film industry. People working on sound, lighting, cameras, research and scripts can switch easily from one area to another.

In February 1988, 1,400 people attended the first Video Communications Festival organised by the newly formed International Visual Communications Association (IVCA). This represents the ranks of the video information business, one of Britain's new growth industries. Its training films are made to the highest professional standards and possess artistic merits in their own right. The stilted training film now belongs to a bygone age. The sight of a surrogate teacher giving instruction to camera has given way to creatively produced mini dramas designed to capture the audience's imagination. Prime examples include *On the Line*, produced for London Underground to show what can happen if you don't stick to the company guidelines on alcohol and drugs at work policy. *Proud and Prejudiced* for Coopers and Lybrand was produced to change attitudes to the role and function of insolvency practice, which may sound boring, but an imaginative treatment with high production values created a great video.

Video is perceived as an effective method of getting information across in the audio-visual age. Lloyds Bank sponsored a new video on money management as an aid to teachers. Videos are now used extensively by medical students. Videos with such exotic titles as *Footcare for Diabetics* and *Flexible Arthroplasty of the Wrist* both had budgets of over £60,000. In 1988, for the first time, BBC Corporate Education produced a video for public sale, as opposed to broadcast.

Demand for a video on AIDS from health agencies in West Germany and Australia led its producer, Lambeth Council, to seek a worldwide distributor. The video was initially launched at a health conference. It was not UK-orientated, carried no commentary and covered problems common to AIDS sufferers everywhere.

The corporate film and video sector consists of approximately 1,500 small companies which in 1991 had a turnover approaching £500 million. Although the industry has suffered in the recession, IVCA believes that this sector is now showing definite signs of recovery. It certainly seems to hold most hope for the future for those now entering, or attempting to enter, the industry.

Business television has also proved a growth area and many multinationals now have a regular weekly satellite programme to inform and train their employees. Ford, BMW, Renault, Volvo and Digital are just a few of the satellite networks, more of which are scheduled for the future.

The sell-through video market has also exploded onto the scene, with many specialist programmes on subjects from yachting to 'lover's guides' and everything in between. Looking towards the near future, the introduction of CD-ROM and interactive multimedia discs can only mean more demand for moving pictures to be seen on a screen.